German

French &

British Political Economy

ISBN: 9781407700496

Published by:
HardPress Publishing
8345 NW 66TH ST #2561
MIAMI FL 33166-2626

Email: info@hardpress.net
Web: http://www.hardpress.net

V. I. LENIN

The
THREE SOURCES
AND THREE
COMPONENT
PARTS
OF MARXISM

Word Cont
2857

V. I. LENIN

THE THREE SOURCES AND THREE COMPONENT PARTS OF MARXISM

KARL MARX

FREDERICK ENGELS

FOREIGN LANGUAGES PUBLISHING HOUSE
MOSCOW

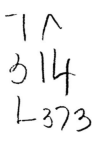

The present issue of Books for Socialism consists of three works by V. I. Lenin—an appreciation of the great teaching of Marx and Engels written at different times. They are: The Three Sources and Three Component Parts of Marxism, Karl Marx, and Frederick Engels. They contain brief biographies of the founders of scientific socialism and list their principal works. They also contain a brief, yet profound, evaluation of the basic aspects of the Marxist theory in all its three component parts, their essence and revolutionary importance.

Along with questions of dialectical and historical materialism and political economy Lenin sets forth the basic principles of scientific socialism. Section III of The Three Sources and Three Component Parts of Marxism is devoted to these principles. In it Lenin renders honour to Marx for developing a truly scientific theory of class struggle and pointing to the proletariat as the social force destined to sweep out the old, and install a new, society.

Lenin's Karl Marx gives an account of the basic problems of the Marxist theory including the key problems of scientific socialism—the socialist revolution and the dictatorship of the proletariat.

In setting out the essence of Marxism, Lenin voiced unshakeable confidence in the ultimate triumph of socialism and the powerful revolutionary potential of the proletariat. He wrote that it was the proletariat which would be the "intellectual and driving force" in the transformation of the old society into a new one. Under socialism there will be a new form of family, new conditions in the status of women and in the upbringing of the younger generation; the national question and the question of the state will be approached in a new way. Lenin deals at length with tactical matters pertinent to the class struggle of the proletariat.

In his Frederick Engels Lenin portrays that great fighter and teacher of the proletariat. Engels collaborated with Marx in developing scientific socialism and proved that socialism is not a vision of dreamers, but a natural and inevitable social phenomenon.

THE EDITORS

CONTENTS

THE THREE SOURCES AND THREE COMPONENT PARTS OF MARXISM[1]

Throughout the civilized world the teachings of Marx evoke the utmost hostility and hatred of all bourgeois science (both official and liberal) which regards Marxism as a kind of "pernicious sect." And no other attitude is to be expected, for there can be no "impartial" social science in a society based on class struggle. In one way or another, *all* official and liberal science *defends* wage slavery, whereas Marxism has declared relentless war on wage slavery. To expect science to be impartial in a wage-slave society is as silly and naive as to expect impartiality from manufacturers on the question whether workers' wages should be increased by decreasing the profits of capital.

But this is not all. The history of philosophy and the history of social science show with perfect clarity that there is nothing resembling "sectarianism" in Marxism, in the sense of its being a hidebound, petrified doctrine, a doctrine which arose *away from* the high road of development of world civilization. On the contrary, the genius of Marx consists precisely in the fact that he furnished answers to questions the foremost minds of mankind had already raised. His teachings arose as the direct and immediate *continuation* of the teachings of the greatest representatives of philosophy, political economy and socialism.

The Marxian doctrine is omnipotent because it is true. It is complete and harmonious, and provides men with an integral world conception which is irreconcilable with any form of superstition, reaction, or defence of bourgeois oppression. It is the legitimate successor to the best that was created by mankind in the nineteenth century in the shape of German philosophy, English political economy and French socialism.

On these three sources of Marxism and on its three component parts, we shall briefly dwell.

I

The philosophy of Marxism is *materialism*. Throughout the modern history of Europe, and especially at the end of the eighteenth century in France, which was the scene of a decisive battle against every kind of medieval rubbish, against feudalism in institutions and ideas, materialism has proved to be the only philosophy that is consistent, true to all the teachings of natural science and hostile to superstition, cant and so forth. The enemies of democracy therefore exerted all their efforts to "refute," undermine and defame materialism, and advocated various forms of philosophical idealism, which always, in one way or another, amounts to an advocacy or support of religion.

Marx and Engels defended philosophical materialism in the most determined manner and repeatedly explained the profound erroneousness of every deviation from this basis. Their views are most clearly and fully expounded in the works of Engels, *Ludwig Feuerbach* and *Anti-Dühring*, which, like the *Communist Manifesto*, are handbooks of every class-conscious worker.

But Marx did not stop at the materialism of the eighteenth century: he advanced philosophy. He enriched it with the acquisitions of German classical philosophy, especially of the Hegelian system, which in its turn led to the materialism of Feuerbach. The chief of these acquisitions is *dialectics*, i.e., the doctrine of development in its fullest and deepest form, free of one-sidedness, the doctrine of the relativity of human knowledge, which provides us with a reflection of eternally developing matter. The latest discoveries of natural science—radium, electrons, the transmutation of elements—have remarkably confirmed Marx's dialectical materialism, despite the teachings of the bourgeois philosophers with their "new" reversions to old and rotten idealism.

Deepening and developing philosophical materialism, Marx completed it, extended its knowledge of nature to the knowledge of *human society*. Marx's *historical materialism* was the greatest achievement of scientific thought. The chaos and arbitrariness that had previously reigned in the views on history and politics gave way to a strikingly integral and harmonious scientific theory, which shows how, in consequence of the growth of productive forces, out of one system of social life another and higher system develops—how capitalism, for instance, grows out of feudalism.

Just as man's knowledge reflects nature (i.e., developing matter) which exists independently of him, so man's *social knowledge* (i.e., his various views and doctrines—philosophical, religious, political and so forth) reflects the *economic system* of society. Political institutions are a superstructure on the economic foundation. We see, for example, that the various political forms of the modern European states serve to fortify the rule of the bourgeoisie over the proletariat.

Marx's philosophy is finished philosophical materialism, which has provided mankind, and especially the working class, with powerful instruments of knowledge.

Having recognized that the economic system is the foundation on which the political superstructure is erected, Marx devoted most attention to the study of this economic system. Marx's principal work, *Capital*, is devoted to a study of the economic system of modern, i.e., capitalist, society.

Classical political economy, before Marx, evolved in England, the most developed of the capitalist countries. Adam Smith and David Ricardo, by their investigations of the economic system, laid the foundations of the *labour theory of value*. Marx continued their work. He rigidly proved and consistently developed this theory. He showed that the value of every commodity is determined by the quantity of socially necessary labour time spent on its production.

Where the bourgeois economists saw a relation between things (the exchange of one commodity for another) Marx revealed a *relation between men*. The exchange of commodities expresses the tie between individual producers through the market. *Money* signifies that this tie is becoming closer and closer, inseparably binding the entire economic life of the individual producers into one whole. *Capital* signifies a further development of this tie: man's labour power becomes a commodity. The wage worker sells his labour power to the owner of the land, factories and instruments of labour. The worker spends one part of the day covering the cost of maintaining himself and his family (wages), while the other part of the day the worker toils without remuneration, creating *surplus value* for the capitalist, the source of profit, the source of the wealth of the capitalist class.

The doctrine of surplus value is the corner-stone of Marx's economic theory.

Capital, created by the labour of the worker, presses on the worker by ruining the small masters and creating an army of unemployed. In industry, the victory of large-scale production is at once apparent, but we observe the same phenomenon in agriculture as well; the superiority of large-scale capitalist agriculture increases, the employment of machinery grows, peasant economy falls into the noose of money-capital, it declines and sinks into ruin under the burden of its backward technique. In agriculture, the decline of small-scale production assumes different forms, but the decline itself is an indisputable fact.

By destroying small-scale production, capital leads to an increase in productivity of labour and to the creation of a monopoly position for the associations of big capitalists. Production itself becomes more and more social—hundreds of thousands and millions of workers become bound together in a systematic economic organism—but the product of the collective labour is appropriated by a handful of capitalists. The anarchy of production grows, as do crises, the furious chase after markets and the insecurity of existence of the mass of the population.

While increasing the dependence of the workers on capital, the capitalist system creates the great power of combined labour.

Marx traced the development of capitalism from the first germs of commodity economy, from simple exchange, to its highest forms, to large-scale production.

And the experience of all capitalist countries, old and new, is clearly demonstrating the truth of this Marxian doctrine to increasing numbers of workers every year.

Capitalism has triumphed all over the world, but this triumph is only the prelude to the triumph of labour over capital.

When feudalism was overthrown, and *"free"* capitalist society appeared on God's earth, it at once became apparent that this freedom meant a new system of oppression and exploitation of the toilers. Various socialist doctrines immediately began to arise as a reflection of and protest against this oppression. But early socialism was *utopian* socialism. It criticized capitalist society, it condemned and damned it, it dreamed of its destruction, it indulged in fancies of a better order and endeavoured to convince the rich of the immorality of exploitation.

But utopian socialism could not point the real way out. It could not explain the essence of wage slavery under capitalism, nor discover the laws of the latter's development, nor point to the *social force* which is capable of becoming the creator of a new society.

Meanwhile, the stormy revolutions which everywhere in Europe, and especially in France, accompanied the fall of feudalism, of serfdom, more and more clearly revealed the *struggle of classes* as the basis and the driving force of all development.

Not a single victory of political freedom over the feudal class was won except against desperate resistance. Not a single capitalist country evolved on a more or less free and democratic basis except by a life and death struggle between the various classes of capitalist society.

The genius of Marx consists in the fact that he was able before anybody else to draw from this and consistently apply the deduction that world history teaches. This deduction is the doctrine of the *class struggle*.

People always were and always will be the stupid victims of deceit and self-deceit in politics until they

learn to discover the *interests* of some class or other
behind all moral, religious, political and social
phrases, declarations and promises._The advocates of
reforms and improvements will always be fooled by the
defenders of the old order until they realize that every
old institution, however barbarous and rotten it may
appear to be, is maintained by the forces of some ruling classes. And there is *only one* way of smashing
the resistance of these classes, and that is to find, in
the very society which surrounds us, and to enlighten
and organize for the struggle, the forces which can—
and, owing to their social position, *must*—constitute
the power capable of sweeping away the old and creating the new.

Marx's philosophical materialism alone has shown
the proletariat the way out of the spiritual slavery in
which all oppressed classes have hitherto languished.
Marx's economic theory alone has explained the true
position of the proletariat in the general system of capitalism.

Independent organizations of the proletariat are
multiplying all over the world, from America to Japan
and from Sweden to South Africa. The proletariat is
becoming enlightened and educated by waging its
class struggle; it is ridding itself of the prejudices of
bourgeois society; it is rallying its ranks ever more
closely and is learning to gauge the measure of its suc-
cesses; it is steeling its forces and is growing irresistibly.

Prosveshcheniye, No. 3,
March 1913
Signed: V. I.

Translated from V. I. Lenin's *Works*,
4th Russ. ed., Vol. 19, pp. 3-8

KARL MARX[2]

(Brief Biographical Sketch with an Exposition of Marxism)

PREFACE

The article on Karl Marx now appearing in a separate printing was written by me in 1913 (as far as I can remember) for the *Granat Encyclopedia*. A rather detailed bibliography of literature on Marx, mostly foreign, was appended at the end of the article. This has been omitted in the present edition. The editors of the *Encyclopedia,* on their part, cut out, for censorship reasons, the end of the article on Marx, namely, the section in which his revolutionary tactics were explained. Unfortunately, I am not in a position to reproduce that end here, because the rough draft remained in my papers somewhere in Cracow or in Switzerland. I only remember that in that concluding part of the article I quoted, among other things, the passage from Marx's letter to Engels of the 16th of April, 1856, where he wrote: "The whole thing in Germany will depend on the possibility to back the proletarian revolution by some second edition of the Peasant War. Then everything will be splendid." That is what our Mensheviks, who have now sunk to utter betrayal of socialism and to desertion to the side of the bourgeoisie, failed to understand in 1905 and after.

N. Lenin

Moscow, May 14, 1918

Published in 1918 in the pamphlet: N. Lenin, *Karl Marx*, Priboi Publishers, Moscow

Translated from V. I. Lenin's *Works,* 4th Russ. ed., Vol. 21, p. 29

Karl Marx was born on May 5, 1818, in the city of Trier (Rhenish Prussia). His father was a lawyer, a Jew, who in 1824 adopted Protestantism. The family was well-to-do, cultured, but not revolutionary. After graduating from the gymnasium in Trier, Marx entered university, first at Bonn and later at Berlin, where he studied jurisprudence, but chiefly history and philosophy. He concluded his course in 1841, submitting his doctoral dissertation on the philosophy of Epicurus. In his views Marx at that time was a Hegelian idealist. In Berlin he belonged to the circle of "Left Hegelians" (Bruno Bauer and others) who sought to draw atheistic and revolutionary conclusions from Hegel's philosophy.

After graduating from the university, Marx moved to Bonn, expecting to become a professor. But the reactionary policy of the government—which in 1832 deprived Ludwig Feuerbach of his chair and in 1836 refused to allow him to return to the uinversity, and in 1841 forbade the young professor Bruno Bauer to lecture at Bonn—forced Marx to abandon the idea of pursuing an academic career. At that time the views of the Left Hegelians were developing very rapidly in Germany. Ludwig Feuerbach, particularly after 1836, began to criticize theology and to turn to materialism, which in 1841 gained the upper hand in his philosophy *(The Essence of Christianity)*; in 1843 his *Principles of the Philosophy of the Future* appeared. "One must himself have experienced the liberating effect" of these books, Engels subsequently wrote of these works of Feuerbach. "We" (i.e., the Left Hegelians, including Marx) "all became at once Feuerbachians." At that time some Rhenish radical bourgeois who had certain points in common with the Left Hegelians founded an opposition paper in Cologne, the *Rheinische Zeitung* (the first number appeared on January 1, 1842). Marx and Bruno Bauer were invited to be the chief contributors, and in October 1842 Marx became chief editor and removed from Bonn to Cologne. The revolutionary-democratic trend of the paper became more and more pronounced under Marx's editorship, and the government first subjected the paper to double and triple censorship and then decided to suppress it altogether on January 1, 1843. Marx had to resign the editorship before that date, but his resignation did not save the paper, which was closed down in March 1843. Of the more important articles contributed by Marx to the *Rheinische Zeitung*, Engels notes, in addition to those indicated below (see *Bibliography*[3]), an article on the condition of the peasant wine-growers of the Moselle Valley. His journalistic activities convinced Marx that he was not sufficiently acquainted with political economy, and he zealously set out to study it.

In 1843, in Kreuznach, Marx married Jenny von Westphalen, a childhood friend to whom he had been engaged while still a student. His wife came from a reactionary family of the Prussian nobility. Her elder brother was Prussian Minister of the Interior at a most reactionary period, 1850-58. In the autumn of 1843 Marx went to Paris in order, together with Arnold Ruge (born 1802, died 1880; a Left Hegelian; in 1825-30, in prison; after 1848, a political exile; after 1866-70, a Bismarckian), to publish a radical magazine abroad.

Only one issue of this magazine, *Deutsch-Französische Jahrbücher*, appeared. It was discontinued owing to the difficulty of secret distribution in Germany and to disagreements with Ruge. In his articles in this magazine Marx already appears as a revolutionary who advocates the "merciless criticism of everything existing," and in particular the "criticism of arms,"[4] and appeals to the *masses* and to the *proletariat*.

In September 1844 Frederick Engels came to Paris for a few days, and from that time forth became Marx's closest friend. They both took a most active part in the then seething life of the revolutionary groups in Paris (of particular importance was Proudhon's doctrine, which Marx thoroughly demolished in his *Poverty of Philosophy*, 1847), and, vigorously combating the various doctrines of petty-bourgeois socialism, worked out the theory and tactics of revolutionary *proletarian socialism*, or communism (Marxism). See Marx's works of this period, 1844-48, in the *Bibliography*. In 1845, on the insistent demand of the Prussian government, Marx was banished from Paris as a dangerous revolutionary. He moved to Brussels. In the spring of 1847 Marx and Engels joined a secret propaganda society called the Communist League;[5] they took a prominent part in the Second Congress of the League (London, November 1847), and at its request drew up the famous *Communist Manifesto*, which appeared in February 1848. With the clarity and brilliance of genius, this work outlines the new world conception, consistent materialism, which also embraces the realm of social life, dialectics, as the most comprehensive and profound doctrine of development, the theory of the class struggle and of the world-historic revolutionary role of the proletariat —the creator of the new, communist society.

When the Revolution of February 1848 broke out, Marx was banished from Belgium. He returned to

Paris, whence, after the March Revolution, he went to Germany, to Cologne. There the *Neue Rheinische Zeitung*⁶ appeared from June 1, 1848, to May 19, 1849; Marx was the chief editor. The new theory was brilliantly corroborated by the course of the revolutionary events of 1848-49, as it has been since corroborated by all proletarian and democratic movements of all countries in the world. The victorious counter-revolution first instigated court proceedings against Marx (he was acquitted on February 9, 1849) and then banished him from Germany (May 16, 1849). Marx first went to Paris, was again banished after the demonstration of June 13, 1849, and then went to London, where he lived to the day of his death.

His life as a political exile was a very hard one, as the correspondence between Marx and Engels (published in 1913) clearly reveals. Marx and his family suffered dire poverty. Were it not for Engels's constant and self-sacrificing financial support, Marx would not only have been unable to finish *Capital* but would have inevitably perished from want. Moreover, the prevailing doctrines and trends of petty-bourgeois socialism, and of non-proletarian socialism in general, forced Marx to carry on a continuous and merciless fight and sometimes to repel the most savage and monstrous personal attacks (*Herr Vogt*). Holding aloof from the circles of political exiles, Marx developed his materialist theory in a number of historic works (see *Bibliography*), devoting his efforts chiefly to the study of political economy. Marx revolutionized this science (see below, "The Marxian Doctrine") in his *Contribution to the Critique of Political Economy* (1859) and *Capital* (Vol. I, 1867).

The period of revival of the democratic movements at the end of the fifties and the sixties recalled Marx to practical activity. In 1864 (September 28) the International Workingmen's Association—the famous First International—was founded in London. Marx was the heart and soul of this organization; he was the author of its first Address and a host of resolutions, declarations and manifestoes. Uniting the labour movement of various countries, striving to direct into the channel of joint activity the various forms of non-proletarian, pre-Marxian socialism (Mazzini, Proudhon, Bakunin, liberal trade unionism in England, Lassallean vacillations to the Right in Germany, etc.), and combating the theories of all these sects and petty schools, Marx hammered out a uniform tactics for the proletarian struggle of the working class in the various countries. After the fall of the Paris Commune (1871)—of which Marx gave such a profound, clear-cut, brilliant and *effective*, revolutionary analysis (*The Civil War in France*, 1871)—and after the International was split by the Bakuninists, the existence of that organization in Europe became impossible. After the Hague Congress of the International (1872) Marx had the General Council of the International transferred to New York. The First International had accomplished its historical role, and it made way for a period of immeasurably larger growth of the labour movement in all the countries of the world, a period, in fact, when the movement grew in *breadth* and when *mass* socialist labour parties in individual national states were created.

His strenuous work in the International and his still more strenuous theoretical occupations completely undermined Marx's health. He continued his work on the reshaping of political economy and the completion of *Capital*, for which he collected a mass of new material and studied a number of languages (Russian, for instance); but ill-health prevented him from finishing *Capital*.

2

On December 2, 1881, his wife died. On March 14, 1883, Marx peacefully passed away in his armchair. He lies buried with his wife in the Highgate Cemetery, London. Of Marx's children some died in childhood in London when the family lived in deep poverty. Three daughters married English and French Socialists: Eleonora Aveling, Laura Lafargue and Jenny Longuet. The latter's son is a member of the French Socialist Party.

THE MARXIAN DOCTRINE

Marxism is the system of the views and teachings of Marx. Marx was the genius who continued and completed the three main ideological currents of the nineteenth century, belonging to the three most advanced countries of mankind: classical German philosophy, classical English political economy, and French socialism together with French revolutionary doctrines in general. The remarkable consistency and integrity of Marx's views, acknowledged even by his opponents, views which in their totality constitute modern materialism and modern scientific socialism, as the theory and programme of the labour movement in all the civilized countries of the world, oblige us to present a brief outline of his world conception in general before proceeding to the exposition of the principal content of Marxism, namely, Marx's economic doctrine.

PHILOSOPHICAL MATERIALISM

From 1844-45, when his views took shape, Marx was a materialist, in particular a follower of L. Feuerbach, whose weak sides he even later considered to consist exclusively in the fact that his materialism was not consistent and comprehensive enough. Marx regarded the historic and "epoch-making" importance of Feuerbach to be that he had resolutely broken away from Hegelian idealism and had proclaimed materialism, which already "in the eighteenth century, especially in France, had been a struggle not only against the existing political institutions and against ... religion and theology, but also ... against all metaphysics" (in the sense of "intoxicated speculation" as distinct from "sober philosophy"). (*The Holy Family*, in the *Literarischer Nachlass.*) "To Hegel..." wrote Marx, "the process of thinking, which, under the name of 'the Idea,' he even transforms into an independent subject, is the demiurgos (the creator, the maker) of the real world.... With me, on the contrary, the ideal is nothing else than the material world reflected by the human mind, and translated into forms of thought." (*Capital*, Vol. I, Afterword to the Second Edition.)[7] In full conformity with this materialist philosophy of Marx's, and expounding it, Frederick Engels wrote in *Anti-Dühring* (which Marx read in manuscript): "The unity of the world does not consist in its being.... The real unity of the world consists in its materiality, and this is proved ... by a long and wearisome development of philosophy and natural science...." "Motion is the mode of existence of matter. Never anywhere has there been matter without motion, or motion without matter, nor can there be.... But if the ... question is raised what thought and consciousness really are and where they come from, it becomes apparent that they are products of the human brain and that man himself is a product of nature, which has developed in and along with its environment; hence it is self-evident that the products of the human brain, being in the last analysis also products of nature, do not contradict the rest of nature's interconnections but are in correspondence with them." "Hegel was an idealist. To him the thoughts within his brain were not the more or less abstract pictures (*Abbilder*, reflections; Engels sometimes speaks of "imprints") of actual things and processes, but, conversely, things and their evolution were only the realized pictures of the 'Idea,' existing somewhere from eternity before the world was."[8] In his *Ludwig Feuerbach*—in which he expounds his and Marx's views on Feuerbach's philosophy, and which he sent to the press after re-reading an old manuscript written by Marx and himself in 1844-45 on Hegel, Feuerbach and the materialist conception of history—Frederick Engels writes: "The great basic question of all philosophy, especially of more recent philosophy, is that concerning the relation of thinking and being, the relation of the spirit and nature ... which is primary, spirit or nature. ... The answers which the philosophers gave to this question split them into two great camps. Those who asserted the primacy of spirit to nature and, therefore, in the last instance, assumed world creation in some form or other ... comprised the camp of idealism. The others, who regarded nature as primary, belong to the various schools of materialism." Any other use of the concepts of (philosophical) idealism and materialism leads only to confusion. Marx decidedly rejected not only idealism, always connected in one way or another with religion, but also the views, especially widespread in our day, of Hume and Kant, agnosticism, criticism, positivism in their various forms, regarding such a philosophy as a "reactionary" concession to idealism and at best a "shamefaced way of surreptitiously accepting materialism, while denying it before the world."[9] On this question, see, in addition to the above-mentioned works of Engels and Marx, a letter of Marx to Engels dated December 12, 1868, in which Marx, referring to an utterance of the well-known naturalist Thomas Huxley that was "more materialistic" than usual, and to his recognition that "as long as we actually observe and think, we cannot possibly get away from materialism,"[10] reproaches him for leaving a "loop-hole" for agnosticism, Humism. It is especially important to note Marx's view on the relation between freedom and necessity: "Freedom is he appreciation of necessity. 'Necessity is blind only in so far as it is not understood.'" (Engels, *Anti-Dühring*.)[11] This means the recognition of objective law in nature and of the dialectical transformation of necessity into freedom (in the same manner as the transformation of the unknown, but knowable, "thing-in-itself" into the "thing-for-us," of the "essence of things" into "phenomena"). Marx and Engels considered the fundamental shortcoming of the "old" materialism, including the materialism of Feuerbach (and still more of the "vulgar" materialism of Büchner, Vogt and Moleschott), to be: (1) that this materialism was "predominantly mechanical," failing to take account of the latest developments of chemistry and biology (in our day it would be necessary to add: and of the electrical theory of matter); (2) that the old materialism was non-historical, non-dialectical (metaphysical, in the sense of anti-dialectical), and did not adhere consistently and comprehensively to the standpoint of development; (3) that it regarded the "human essence" abstractly and not as the "ensemble" of all (concretely defined historical) "social relations," and therefore only "interpreted" the world, whereas the point is to "change" it; that is to say, it did not understand the importance of "revolutionary, practical activity."[12]

DIALECTICS

Hegelian dialectics, as the most comprehensive, the most rich in content, and the most profound doctrine of development, was regarded by Marx and Engels as the greatest achievement of classical German philosophy. They considered every other formulation of the principle of development, of evolution, one-sided and poor in content, and distorting and mutilating the real course of development (which often proceeds by leaps, catastrophes and revolutions) in nature and in society. "Marx and I were pretty well the only people to rescue conscious dialectics" (from the destruction of idealism, including Hegelianism) "and apply it in the materialist conception of nature.... Nature is the proof of dialectics, and it must be said for modern natural science that it has furnished this proof with very rich materials" (this was written before the discovery of radium, electrons, the transmutation of elements, etc.!) "increasing daily, and thus has shown that, in the last resort, nature works dialectically and not metaphysically."[13]

"The great basic thought," Engels writes, "that the world is not to be comprehended as a complex of ready-made things, but as a complex of processes, in which the things apparently stable no less than their mind images in our heads, the concepts, go through an uninterrupted change of coming into being and passing away ... this great fundamental thought has, especially since the time of Hegel, so thoroughly permeated ordinary consciousness that in this generality it is now scarcely ever contradicted. But to acknowledge this fundamental thought in words and to apply it in reality in detail to each domain of investigation are two different things." "For dialectical philosophy nothing is final, absolute, sacred. It reveals the transitory character of everything and in everything; nothing can endure before it except the uninterrupted process of becoming and of passing away, of endless ascendency from the lower to the higher. And dialectical philosophy itself is nothing more than the mere reflection of this process in the thinking brain." Thus, according to Marx, dialectics is "the science of the general laws of motion, both of the external world and of human thought."[14]

This revolutionary side of Hegel's philosophy was adopted and developed by Marx. Dialectical materialism "no longer needs any philosophy standing above the other sciences." Of former philosophy there remains "the science of thought and its laws—formal logic and dialectics."[15] And dialectics, as understood by Marx, and in conformity with Hegel, includes what is now called the theory of knowledge, or epistemology, which, too, must regard its subject matter historically, studying and generalizing the origin and development of knowledge, the transition from *non*-knowledge to knowledge.

Nowadays, the idea of development, of evolution, has penetrated the social consciousness almost in its entirety, but by different ways, not by way of the Hegelian philosophy. But as formulated by Marx and Engels on the basis of Hegel, this idea is far more comprehensive, far richer in content than the current idea of evolution. A development that seemingly repeats the stages already passed, but repeats them otherwise, on a higher basis ("negation of negation"), a development, so to speak, in spirals, not in a straight line; —a development by leaps, catastrophes, revolutions; —"breaks in continuity"; the transformation of quantity into quality; —the inner impulses to development, imparted by the contradiction and conflict of the various forces and tendencies acting on a given body, or within a given phenomenon, or within a given society;— the interdependence and the closest, indissoluble connexion of *all* sides of every phenomenon (while history constantly discloses ever new sides), a connexion that provides a uniform, law-governed, universal process of motion—such are some of the features of dialectics as a richer (than the ordinary) doctrine of development. (Cf. Marx's letter to Engels of January 8, 1868, in which he ridicules Stein's "wooden trichotomies" which it would be absurd to confuse with materialist dialectics.)

THE MATERIALIST CONCEPTION OF HISTORY

Having realized the inconsistency, incompleteness, and one-sidedness of the old materialism, Marx became convinced of the necessity of "bringing the science of society . . . into harmony with the materialist foundation, and of reconstructing it thereupon."[16] Since materialism in general explains consciousness as the outcome of being, and not conversely, materialism as applied to the social life of mankind has to explain *social* consciousness as the outcome of *social* being. "Technology," writes Marx (*Capital*, Vol. I), "discloses man's mode of dealing with nature, the process of production by which he sustains his life, and thereby also lays bare the mode of formation of his social relations, and of the mental conceptions that flow from them."[17] In the preface to his *Contribution to the Critique of Political Economy*, Marx gives an integral formulation of the fundamental principles of materialism as extended to human society and its history, in the following words:

"In the social production of their life, men enter into definite relations that are indispensable and independent of their will, relations of production which correspond to a definite stage of development of their material productive forces.

"The sum-total of these relations of production constitutes the economic structure of society, the real foundation, on which rises a legal and political superstructure and to which correspond definite forms of social consciousness. The mode of production of material life conditions the social, political and intellectual life process in general. It is not the consciousness of men that determines their being, but, on the contrary, their social being that determines their consciousness. At a certain stage of their development, the material productive forces of society come in conflict with the existing relations of production, or—what is but a legal expression for the same thing—with the property relations within which they have been at work hitherto. From forms of development of the productive forces these relations turn into their fetters. Then begins an epoch of social revolution. With the change of the economic foundation the entire immense superstructure is more or less rapidly transformed. In considering such transformations a distinction should always be made between the material transformation of the economic conditions of production, which can be determined with the precision of natural science, and the legal, political, religious, esthetic or philosophic—in short, ideological forms in which men become conscious of this conflict and fight it out.

"Just as our opinion of an individual is not based on what he thinks of himself, so can we not judge of such a period of transformation by its own consciousness; on the contrary, this consciousness must be explained rather from the contradictions of material life, from the existing conflict between the social productive forces and the relations of production. . . . In broad outlines Asiatic, ancient, feudal, and modern bourgeois modes of production can be designated as progressive epochs in the economic formation of society."[18] (Cf. Marx's brief formulation in a letter to Engels dated July 7, 1866: "Our theory that the organization of labour is determined by the means of production."[19])

27

The discovery of the materialist conception of history, or rather, the consistent continuation and extension of materialism into the domain of social phenomena, removed two chief defects of earlier historical theories. In the first place, they at best examined only the ideological motives of the historical activity of human beings, without investigating what produced these motives, without grasping the objective laws governing the development of the system of social relations, and without discerning the roots of these relations in the degree of development of material production; in the second place, the earlier theories did not cover the activities of the *masses* of the population, whereas historical materialism made it possible for the first time to study with the accuracy of the natural sciences the social conditions of the life of the masses and the changes in these conditions. Pre-Marxian "sociology" and historiography *at best* provided an accumulation of raw facts, collected sporadically, and a depiction of certain sides of the historical process. By examining the whole *complex* of opposing tendencies, by reducing them to precisely definable conditions of life and production of the various *classes* of society, by discarding subjectivism and arbitrariness in the choice of various "leading" ideas or in their interpretation, and by disclosing that all ideas and all the various tendencies, without exception, have their *roots* in the condition of the material forces of production, Marxism pointed the way to an all-embracing and comprehensive study of the process of rise, development, and decline of social-economic formations. People make their own history. But what determines the motives of people, of the mass of people, that is; what gives rise to the clash of conflicting ideas and strivings; what is the sum-total of all these clashes of the whole mass of human societies; what are the objective conditions of production of material life that form the basis of all historical activity of man; what is the law of development of these conditions—to all this Marx drew attention and pointed out the way to a scientific study of history as a uniform and law-governed process in all its immense variety and contradictoriness.

THE CLASS STRUGGLE

That in any given society the strivings of some of its members conflict with the strivings of others, that social life is full of contradictions, that history discloses a struggle between nations and societies as well as within nations and societies, and, in addition, an alternation of periods of revolution and reaction, peace and war, stagnation and rapid progress or decline—are facts that are generally known. Marxism provided the clue which enables us to discover the laws governing this seeming labyrinth and chaos, namely, the theory of the class struggle. Only a study of the whole complex of strivings of all the members of a given society or group of societies can lead to a scientific definition of the result of these strivings. And the source of the conflicting strivings lies in the difference in the position and mode of life of the *classes* into which each society is divided. "The history of all hitherto existing society is the history of class struggles," wrote Marx in the *Communist Manifesto* (except the history of the primitive community—Engels added subsequently). "Freeman and slave, patrician and plebeian, lord and serf, guildmaster and journeyman, in a word, oppressor and oppressed, stood in constant opposition to one another, carried on an uninterrupted, now hidden, now open fight, a fight that each time ended, either in a revolutionary reconstitution of society at large, or in the common ruin of the contending classes.... The modern bourgeois society that has sprouted from the ruins of feudal society has not done away with class antagonisms. It has but established new classes, new conditions of oppression, new forms of struggle in place of the old ones. Our epoch, the epoch of the bourgeoisie, possesses, however, this distinctive feature: it has simplified the class antagonisms. Society as a whole is more and more splitting up into two great hostile camps, into two great classes directly facing each other: Bourgeoisie and Proletariat." Ever since the Great French Revolution, European history has very clearly revealed in a number of countries this real undersurface of events, the struggle of classes. And the Restoration period in France already produced a number of historians (Thierry, Guizot, Mignet, Thiers) who, generalizing from events, were forced to recognize that the class struggle was the key to all French history. And the modern era—the era of the complete victory of the bourgeoisie, representative institutions, wide (if not universal) suffrage, a cheap, popular daily press, etc., the era of powerful and ever-expanding unions of workers and unions of employers, etc., has revealed even more manifestly (though sometimes in a very one-sided, "peaceful," "constitutional" form) that the class struggle is the mainspring of events. The following passage from Marx's *Communist Manifesto* will show us what Marx required of social science in respect to an objective analysis of the position of each class in modern society in connexion with an analysis of the conditions of development of each class: "Of all the classes that stand face to face with the bourgeoisie today, the proletariat alone is a really revolutionary class. The other classes decay and finally disappear in the face of modern industry; the proletariat is its special and essential product. The lower middle class, the small manufacturer, the shopkeeper, the artisan, the peasant, all these fight against the bourgeoisie, to save from extinction their existence as fractions of the middle class. They are therefore not revolutionary, but conservative. Nay more, they are reactionary, for they try to roll back the wheel of history. If by chance they are revolutionary, they are so only in view of their impending transfer into the proletariat, they thus defend not their present, but their future interests, they desert their own standpoint to place themselves at that of the proletariat."[20] In a number of historical works (see *Bibliography*), Marx has given us brilliant and profound examples of materialist historiography, of an analysis of the position of *each* individual class, and sometimes of various groups or strata within a class, showing plainly why and how "every class struggle is a political struggle."[21] The above-quoted passage is an illustration of what a complex network of social relations and *transitional* stages between one class and another, from the past to the future, Marx analyzes in order to determine the resultant of historical development.

The most profound, comprehensive and detailed confirmation and application of Marx's theory is his economic doctrine.

MARX'S ECONOMIC DOCTRINE

"It is the ultimate aim of this work, to lay bare the economic law of motion of modern society" (that is to say, capitalist, bourgeois society), says Marx in the preface to *Capital*.[22] The investigation of the relations of production in a given, historically defined society, in their genesis, development, and decline—such is the content of Marx's economic doctrine. In capitalist society it is the production of *commodities* that dominates, and Marx's analysis therefore begins with an analysis of the commodity.

A commodity is, in the first place, a thing that satis-
fies a human want; in the second place, it is a thing
that can be exchanged for another thing. The utility of
a thing makes it a *use-value*. Exchange-value (or simply, value) presents itself first of all as the ratio, the
proportion in which a certain number of use-values of
one sort are exchanged for a certain number of use-
values of another sort. Daily experience shows us that
millions upon millions of such exchanges are constantly equating one with another every kind of use-value,
even the most diverse and incomparable. Now, what
is there in common between these various things,
things constantly equated one with another in a definite system of social relations? What is common to
them is that they are *products of labour*. In exchanging products people equate to one another the most
diverse kinds of labour. The production of commodities
is a system of social relations in which the individual
producers create diverse products (the social division
of labour), and in which all these products are equated
to one another in exchange. Consequently, what is common to all commodities is not the concrete labour of a
definite branch of production, not labour of one particular kind, but *abstract* human labour—human labour
in general. All the labour power of a given society, as
represented in the sum-total of values of all commodities, is one and the same human labour power: millions
and millions of acts of exchange prove this. And, consequently, each particular commodity represents only
a certain share of the *socially necessary* labour time.
The magnitude of value is determined by the amount of
socially necessary labour, or by the labour time that is
socially necessary for the production of the given commodity, of the given use-value. "Whenever, by an ex-

change, we equate as values our different products, by that very act, we also equate, as human labour, the different kinds of labour expended upon them. We are not aware of this, nevertheless we do it."[23] As one of the earlier economists said, value is a relation between two persons; only he ought to have added: a relation disguised as a relation between things. We can understand what value is only when we consider it from the standpoint of the system of social relations of production of one particular historical formation of society, relations, moreover, which manifest themselves in the mass phenomenon of exchange, a phenomenon which repeats itself millions upon millions of times. "As values, all commodities are only definite masses of congealed labour time."[24] Having made a detailed analysis of the twofold character of the labour incorporated in commodities, Marx goes on to analyze the *forms of value* and *money*. Marx's main task here is to study the *genesis* of the money form of value, to study the *historical process* of development of exchange, from single and casual acts of exchange ("elementary or accidental form of value," in which a given quantity of one commodity is exchanged for a given quantity of another) to the universal form of value, in which a number of different commodities are exchanged for one and the same particular commodity, and to the money form of value, when gold becomes this particular commodity, the universal equivalent. Being the highest product of the development of exchange and commodity production, money masks and conceals the social character of all individual labour, the social tie between the individual producers who are united by the market. Marx analyzes in very great detail the various functions of money; and it is essential to note here in particular (as generally in the opening chapters of *Capital*), that the abstract and seemingly at times purely deductive mode of exposition in reality reproduces a gigantic collection of factual material on the history of the development of exchange and commodity production. "If we consider money, its existence implies a definite stage in the exchange of commodities. The particular functions of money which it performs, either as the mere equivalent of commodities, or as means of circulation, or means of payment, as hoard or as universal money, point, according to the extent and relative preponderance of the one function or the other, to very different stages in the process of social production." (*Capital*, Vol. I.)[25]

SURPLUS VALUE

At a certain stage in the development of commodity production money becomes transformed into capital. The formula of commodity circulation was C—M—C (commodity—money—commodity), i.e., the sale of one commodity for the purpose of buying another. The general formula of capital, on the contrary, is M—C—M, i.e., purchase for the purpose of selling (at a profit). The increase over the original value of the money put into circulation Marx calls surplus value. The fact of this "growth" of money in capitalist circulation is well known. It is this "growth" which transforms money into *capital*, as a special, historically defined, social relation of production. Surplus value cannot arise out of commodity circulation, for the latter knows only the exchange of equivalents; it cannot arise out of an addition to price, for the mutual losses and gains of buyers and sellers would equalize one another, whereas what we have here is not an individual phenomenon but a mass, average, social phenomenon. In order to derive surplus value, the owner of money "must ... find ... in the market a commodity, whose use-value possesses the peculiar property of being a source of value"[26]—a commodity whose process of consumption is at the same time a process of creation of value. And such a commodity exists. It is human labour power. Its consumption is labour, and labour creates value. The owner of money buys labour power at its value, which, like the value of every other commodity, is determined by the socially necessary labour time requisite for its production (i.e., the cost of maintaining the worker and his family). Having bought labour power, the owner of money is entitled to use it, that is, to set it to work for the whole day—twelve hours, let us suppose. Yet, in the course of six hours ("necessary" labour time) the labourer creates product sufficient to cover the cost of his own maintenance; and in the course of the next six hours ("surplus" labour time), he creates "surplus" product, or surplus value, for which the capitalist does not pay. In capital, therefore, from the standpoint of the process of production, two parts must be distinguished: constant capital, expended on means of production (machinery, tools, raw materials, etc.), the value of which, without any change, is transferred (all at once or part by part) to the finished product; and variable capital, expended on labour power. The value of this latter capital is not invariable, but grows in the labour process, creating surplus value. Therefore, to express the degree of exploitation of labour power by capital, surplus value must be compared not with the whole capital but only with the variable capital. Thus in the example given, the rate of surplus value, as Marx calls this ratio, will be 6:6, i.e., 100 per cent.

The historical prerequisites for the genesis of capital were, firstly, the accumulation of a certain sum of money in the hands of individuals and a relatively high level of development of commodity production in general, and secondly, the existence of a labourer who is "free" in a double sense: free from all constraint or restriction on the sale of his labour power, and free from the land and all means of production in general, a free and unattached labourer, a "proletarian," who cannot subsist except by the sale of his labour power.

There are two principal methods by which surplus value can be increased: by lengthening the working day ("absolute surplus value"), and by shortening the necessary working day ("relative surplus value"). Analyzing the first method, Marx gives a most impressive picture of the struggle of the working class to shorten the working day and of governmental interference to lengthen the working day (from the fourteenth century to the seventeenth century) and to shorten the working day (factory legislation of the nineteenth century). Since the appearance of *Capital*, the history of the working-class movement in all civilized countries of the world has provided a wealth of new facts amplifying this picture.

Analyzing the production of relative surplus value, Marx investigates the three main historical stages by which capitalism has increased the productivity of labour: 1) simple co-operation; 2) division of labour and manufacture; 3) machinery and large-scale industry. How profoundly Marx has here revealed the basic and typical features of capitalist development is incidentally shown by the fact that investigations of what is known as the "kustar" industry of Russia furnish abundant material illustrating the first two of the mentioned stages. And the revolutionizing effect of large-scale machine industry, described by Marx in 1867, has been revealed in a number of "new" countries (Russia, Japan, etc.) in the course of the half-century that has since elapsed.

To continue. New and important in the highest degree is Marx's analysis of the *accumulation of capital,* i.e., the transformation of a part of surplus value into capital, its use, not for satisfying the personal needs or whims of the capitalist, but for new production. Marx revealed the mistake of all the earlier classical political economists (from Adam Smith on) who assumed that the entire surplus value which is transformed into capital goes to form variable capital. In actual fact, it is divided into *means of production* and variable capital. Of tremendous importance to the process of development of capitalism and its transformation into socialism is the more rapid growth of the constant capital share (of the total capital) as compared with the variable capital share.

The accumulation of capital, by accelerating the supplanting of workers by machinery and creating wealth at one pole and poverty at the other, also gives rise to what is called the "reserve army of labour," to the "relative surplus" of workers, or "capitalist overpopulation," which assumes the most diverse forms and enables capital to expand production at an extremely fast rate. This, in conjunction with credit facilities and the accumulation of capital in means of production, incidentally furnishes the clue to the *crises* of over-production that occurred periodically in capitalist countries—at first at an average of every ten years, and later at more lengthy and less definite intervals. From the accumulation of capital under capitalism must be distinguished what is known as primitive accumulation: the forcible divorcement of the worker from the means of production, the driving of the peasants from the land, the stealing of the commons, the system of colonies and national debts, protective tariffs, and the like. "Primitive accumulation" creates the "free" proletarian at one pole, and the owner of money, the capitalist, at the other.

The *"historical tendency of capitalist accumulation"* is described by Marx in the following famous words: "The expropriation of the immediate producers is accomplished with merciless vandalism, and under the stimulus of passions the most infamous, the most sordid, the pettiest, the most meanly odious. Self-earned private property" (of the peasant and handicraftsman), "that is based, so to say, on the fusing together of the isolated, independent labouring-individual with the conditions of his labour, is supplanted by capitalistic private property, which rests on exploitation of the nominally free labour of others. . . . That which is now to be expropriated is no longer the labourer working for himself, but the capitalist exploiting many labourers. This expropriation is accomplished by the action of the immanent laws of capitalistic production itself, by the centralization of capital. One capitalist always kills many. Hand in hand with this centralization, or this expropriation of many capitalists by few, develop, on an ever extending scale, the co-operative form of the labour process, the conscious technical application of science, the methodical cultivation of the soil, the transformation of the instruments of labour into instruments of labour only usable in common, the economizing of all means of production by their use as the means of production of combined, socialized labour, the entanglement of all peoples in the net of the world market, and with this, the international character of the capitalistic regime. Along with the constantly diminishing number of the magnates of capital, who usurp and monopolize all advantages of this process of transformation, grows the mass of misery, oppression, slavery, degradation, exploitation; but with this too grows the revolt of the working class, a class always increasing in numbers, and disciplined, united, organized by the very mechanism of the process of capitalist production itself. The monopoly of capital becomes a fetter upon the mode of production, which has sprung up and flourished along with, and under it. Centralization of the means of production and socialization of labour at last reach a point where they become incompatible with their capitalist integument. Thus integument is burst asunder. The knell of capitalist private property sounds. The expropriators are expropriated." (*Capital*, Vol. I.)[27]

New and important in the highest degree, further, is the analysis Marx gives in the second volume of *Capital* of the reproduction of the aggregate social capital. Here, too, Marx deals not with an individual phenomenon but with a mass phenomenon; not with a fractional part of the economy of society but with this economy as a whole. Correcting the mistake of the classical economists mentioned above, Marx divides the entire social production into two big sections: I) production of means of production, and II) production of articles of consumption, and examines in detail, with arithmetical examples, the circulation of the aggregate social capital—both in the case of reproduction in its former dimensions and in the case of accumulation. The third volume of *Capital* solves the problem of the formation of the *average rate of profit* on the basis of the law of value. The immense advance in economic science made by Marx consists in the fact that he conducts his analysis from the standpoint of mass economic phenomena, of the social economy as a whole, and not from the standpoint of individual cases or of the external, superficial aspects of competition, to which vulgar political economy and the modern "theory of marginal utility" are frequently limited. Marx first analyzes the origin of surplus value, and then goes on to consider its division into profit, interest, and ground rent. Profit is the ratio between the surplus value and the total capital invested in an undertaking. Capital with a "high organic composition" (i.e., with a preponderance of constant capital over variable capital exceeding the social average) yields a lower than average rate of profit; capital with a "low organic composition" yields a higher than average rate of profit. The competition of capitals, and the freedom with which they transfer from one branch to another equate the rate of profit to the average in both cases. The sum-total of the values of all the commodities of a given society coincides with the sum-total of prices of the commodities; but, owing to competition, in individual undertakings and branches of production commodities are sold not at their values but at the *prices of production* (or production prices), which are equal to the expended capital plus the average profit.

In this way the well-known and indisputable fact of the divergence between prices and values and of the equalization of profits is fully explained by Marx on the basis of the law of value; for the sum-total of values of all commodities coincides with the sum-total of prices. However, the equation of (social) value to (individual) prices does not take place simply and directly, but in a very complex way. It is quite natural that in a society of separate producers of commodities, who are united only by the market, law can reveal itself only as an average, social, mass law, when individual deviations to one side or the other mutually compensate one another.

An increase in the productivity of labour implies a more rapid growth of constant capital as compared with variable capital. And since surplus value is a function of variable capital alone, it is obvious that the rate of profit (the ratio of surplus value to the whole capital, and not to its variable part alone) tends to fall.

Marx makes a detailed analysis of this tendency and of a number of circumstances that conceal or counteract it. Without pausing to give an account of the extremely interesting sections of the third volume of *Capital* devoted to usurer's capital, commercial capital and money capital, we pass to the most important section, the theory of *ground rent*. Owing to the fact that the land area is limited and, in capitalist countries, is all occupied by individual private owners, the price of production of agricultural products is determined by the cost of production not on average soil, but on the worst soil, not under average conditions, but under the worst conditions of delivery of produce to the market. The difference between this price and the price of production on better soil (or under better conditions) constitutes *differential* rent. Analyzing this in detail, and showing how it arises out of the difference in fertility of different plots of land and the difference in the amount of capital invested in land, Marx fully exposed (see also *Theories of Surplus-Value*, in which the criticism of Rodbertus deserves particular attention) the error of Ricardo, who considered that differential rent is derived only when there is a successive transition from better land to worse. On the contrary, there may be inverse transitions, land may pass from one category into others (owing to advances in agricultural technique, the growth of towns, and so on), and the notorious "law of diminishing returns" is a profound error which charges nature with the defects, limitations and contradictions of capitalism. Further, the equalization of profit in all branches of industry and national economy in general presupposes complete freedom of competition and the free flow of capital from one branch to another. But the private ownership of land creates monopoly, which hinders this free flow. Owing to this monopoly, the products of agriculture, which is distinguished by a lower organic composition of capital, and, consequently, by an individually higher rate of profit, do not participate in the entirely free process of equalization of the rate of profit; the landowner, being a monopolist, can keep the price above the average, and this monopoly price engenders *absolute* rent. Differential rent cannot be done away with under capitalism, but absolute rent *can*—for instance, by the nationalization of the land, by making it the property of the state. Making the land the property of the state would undermine the monopoly of private landowners, and would lead to a more systematic and complete application of freedom of competition in the domain of agriculture. And, therefore, Marx points out, in the course of history bourgeois radicals have again and again advanced this progressive bourgeois demand for the nationalization of the land, which, however, frightens away the majority of the bourgeoisie, because it too closely "touches" another monopoly, which is particularly important and "sensitive" in our day—the monopoly of the means of production in general. (Marx gives a remarkably popular, concise, and clear exposition of his theory of the average rate of profit on capital and of absolute ground rent in a letter to Engels dated August 2, 1862. See *Briefwechsel*, Vol. III, pp. 77-81; also the letter of August 9, 1862, *ibid.*, pp. 86-87.[28])—For the history of ground rent it is also important to note Marx's analysis showing how labour rent (when the peasant creates surplus product by labouring on the lord's land) is transformed into rent in produce or in kind (when the peasant creates surplus product on his own land and cedes it to the lord due to "non-economic constraint"), then into money rent (which is rent in kind transformed into money, the "obrok" of the old Russia, due to the development of commodity production), and finally into capitalist rent, when the peasant is replaced by the agricultural entrepreneur, who cultivates the soil with the help of wage labour. In connexion with this analysis of the "genesis of capitalist ground rent," note should be made of a number of penetrating ideas (especially important for backward countries like Russia) expressed by Marx on the *evolution of capitalism in agriculture.* "The transformation of rent in kind into money rent is not only necessarily accompanied, but even anticipated by the formation of a class of propertyless day labourers, who hire themselves out for wages. During the period of their rise, when this new class appears but sporadically, the custom necessarily develops among the better-situated tributary farmers of exploiting agricultural labourers for their own account, just as the wealthier serfs in feudal times used to employ serfs for their own benefit. In this way they gradually acquire the ability to accumulate a certain amount of wealth and to transform themselves even into future capitalists. The old self-employing possessors of the land thus give rise among themselves to a nursery for capitalist tenants, whose development is conditioned upon the general development of capitalist production outside of the rural districts." (*Capital*, Vol. III, p. 332.)[29] "The expropriation and eviction of a part of the agricultural population not only set free for industrial capital the labourers, their means of subsistence, and material for labour; it also created the home market." (*Capital*, Vol. I, p. 778.) The impoverishment and ruin of the agricultural population lead, in their turn, to the formation of a reserve army of labour for capital. In every capitalist country "part of the agricultural population is therefore constantly on the point of passing over into an urban or manufacturing proletariat.... (Manufacture is used here in the sense of all non-agricultural industries.) This source of relative surplus population is thus constantly flowing. . . . The agricultural labourer is therefore reduced to the minimum of wages, and always stands with one foot already in the swamp of pauperism." (*Capital*, Vol. I, p. 668.)[30] The private ownership of the peasant in the land he tills constitutes the basis of small-scale production and the condition for its prospering and attaining a classical form. But such small-scale production is compatible only with a narrow and primitive framework of production and society. Under capitalism the "exploitation of the peasants differs only in form from the exploitation of the industrial proletariat. The exploiter is the same: capital. The individual capitalists exploit the individual peasants through mortgages and usury; the capitalist class exploits the peasant class through the state taxes." (*The Class Struggles in France*.) "The small holding of the peasant is now only the pretext that allows the capitalist to draw profits, interest and rent from the soil, while leaving it to the tiller of the soil himself to see how he can extract his wages." (*The Eighteenth Brumaire*.) As a rule the peasant cedes to capitalist society, i.e., to the capitalist class, even a part of the wages, sinking "to the level of the Irish tenant farmer—all under the pretence of being a private proprietor." (*The Class Struggles in France*.) What is "one of the causes which keeps the price of cereals lower in countries with a predominance of small farmers than in countries with a capitalist mode of production"? (*Capital*, Vol. III, p. 340.) It is that the peasant cedes to society (i.e., to the capitalist class) part of his surplus product without an equivalent. "This lower price (of cereals and other agricultural produce) is also a result of the poverty of the producers and by no means of the productivity of their labour." (*Capital*, Vol. III, p. 340.) The small-holding system, which is the normal form of small-scale production, deteriorates, collapses, perishes under capitalism. "Small peasants' property excludes by its very nature the development of the social powers of production of labour, the social forms of labour, the social concentration of capitals, cattle raising on a large scale, and a progressive application of science. Usury and a system of taxation must impoverish it everywhere. The expenditure of capital in the price of the land withdraws this capital from cultivation. An infinite dissipation of means of production and an isolation of the producers themselves go with it." (Co-operative societies, i.e., associations of small peasants, while playing an extremely progressive bourgeois role, only weaken this tendency without eliminating it; nor must it be forgotten that these co-operative societies do much for the well-to-do peasants, and very little, almost nothing, for the mass of poor peasants; and then the associations themselves become exploiters of wage labour.) "Also an enormous waste of human energy. A progressive deterioration of the conditions of production and a raising of the price of means of production is a necessary law of small peasants' property."[31] In agriculture, as in industry, capitalism transforms the process of production only at the price of the "martyrdom of the producer." "The dispersion of the rural labourers over larger areas breaks their power of resistance while concentration increases that of the town operatives. In modern agriculture, as in the urban industries, the increased productiveness and quantity of the labour set in motion are bought at the cost of laying waste and consuming by disease labour power itself. Moreover, all progress in capitalistic agriculture is a progress in the art, not only of robbing the labourer, but of robbing the soil. . . . Capitalist production, therefore, develops technology, and the combining together of various processes into a social whole, only by sapping the original sources of all wealth—the soil and the labourer." (*Capital*, Vol. I, end of Chap. 13.)[32]

SOCIALISM

From the foregoing it is evident that Marx deduces the inevitability of the transformation of capitalist society into socialist society wholly and exclusively from the economic law of motion of contemporary society. The socialization of labour, which is advancing ever more rapidly in thousands of forms, and which has manifested itself very strikingly during the half-century that has elapsed since the death of Marx in the growth of large-scale production, capitalist cartels, syndicates and trusts, as well as in the gigantic increase in the dimensions and power of finance capital, forms the chief material foundation for the inevitable coming of socialism. The intellectual and moral driving force and the physical executant of this transformation is the proletariat, which is trained by capitalism itself. The struggle of the proletariat against the bourgeoisie, which manifests itself in various and, as to its content, increasingly multifarious forms, inevitably becomes a political struggle aiming at the conquest of political power by the proletariat ("the dictatorship of the proletariat"). The socialization of production is bound to lead to the conversion of the means of production into the property of society, to the "expropriation of the expropriators." This conversion will directly result in an immense increase in productivity of labour, a reduction of working hours, and the replacement of the remnants, the ruins of small-scale, primitive, disunited production by collective and improved labour. Capitalism finally snaps the bond between agriculture and industry; but at the same time, in its highest development it prepares new elements of this bond, of a union between industry and agriculture based on the conscious application of science and the combination of collective labour, and on a redistribution of the human population (putting an end at one and the same time to rural remoteness, isolation and barbarism, and to the unnatural concentration of vast masses of people in big cities). A new form of family, new conditions in the status of women and in the upbringing of the younger generation are being prepared by the highest forms of modern capitalism: female and child labour and the break-up of the patriarchal family by capitalism inevitably assume the most terrible, disastrous, and repulsive forms in modern society. Nevertheless "...modern industry, by assigning as it does an important part in the process of production, outside the domestic sphere, to women, to young persons, and to children of both sexes, creates a new economic foundation for a higher form of the family and of the relations between the sexes. It is, of course, just as absurd to hold the Teutonic-Christian form of the family to be absolute and final as it would be to apply that character to the ancient Roman, the ancient Greek, or the Eastern forms which, moreover, taken together form a series in historic development. Moreover, it is obvious that the fact of the collective working group being composed of individuals of both sexes and all ages, must necessarily, under suitable conditions, become a source of humane development; although in its spontaneously developed, brutal, capitalistic form, where the labourer exists for the process of production, and not the process of production for the labourer, that fact is a pestiferous source of corruption and slavery." (*Capital*, Vol. I, end of Chap. 13.) In the factory system is to be found "the germ of the education of the future, an education that will, in the case of every

47

child over a given age, combine productive labour with instruction and gymnastics, not only as one of the methods of adding to the efficiency of production, but as the only method of producing fully developed human beings." (*Ibid.*)[33] Marxian socialism puts the question of nationality and of the state on the same historical footing, not only in the sense of explaining the past but also in the sense of a fearless forecast of the future and of bold practical action for its achievement. Nations are an inevitable product, an inevitable form in the bourgeois epoch of social development. The working class could not grow strong, could not become mature and formed without "constituting itself within the nation," without being "national" ("though not in the bourgeois sense of the word"). But the development of capitalism more and more breaks down national barriers, destroys national seclusion, substitutes class antagonisms for national antagonisms. It is, therefore, perfectly true that in the developed capitalist countries "the workingmen have no country" and that "united action" of the workers, of the civilized countries at least, "is one of the first conditions for the emancipation of the proletariat." (*Communist Manifesto.*) The state, which is organized violence, inevitably came into being at a definite stage in the development of society, when society had split into irreconcilable classes, and when it could not exist without an "authority" ostensibly standing above society and to a certain degree separate from society. Arising out of class contradictions, the state becomes ". . . the state of the most powerful, economically dominant class, which, through the medium of the state, becomes also the politically dominant class, and thus acquires new means of holding down and exploiting the oppressed class. Thus, the state of antiquity was above all the state of the slave owners for the purpose of holding down the slaves, as the feudal state was the organ of the nobility for holding down the peasant serfs and bondsmen, and the modern representative state is an instrument of exploitation of wage labour by capital." (Engels, *The Origin of the Family, Private Property and the State*, a work in which the writer expounds his own and Marx's views.) Even the freest and most progressive form of the bourgeois state, the democratic republic, in no way removes this fact, but merely changes its form (connexion between the government and the stock exchange, corruption—direct and indirect—of the officialdom and the press, etc.). Socialism, by leading to the abolition of classes, will thereby lead to the abolition of the state. "The first act," writes Engels in *Anti-Dühring*, "by virtue of which the state really constitutes itself the representative of the whole of society—the taking possession of the means of production in the name of society—this is, at the same time, its last independent act as a state. State interference in social relations becomes, in one domain after another, superfluous and then dies out of itself; the government of .persons is replaced by the administration of things, and by the conduct of processes of production. The state is not 'abolished.' It dies out."[34] "The society that will organize production on the basis of a free and equal association of the producers will put the whole machinery of state where it will then belong: into the museum of antiquities, by the side of the spinning wheel and the bronze axe." (Engels, *The Origin of the Family, Private Property and the State*.)

Finally, as regards the attitude of Marxian socialism towards the small peasantry, which will continue to exist in the period of the expropriation of the expropriators, we must refer to a declaration made by Engels which expresses Marx's views: "... when we are in possession of state power we shall not even think of forcibly expropriating the small peasants (regardless of whether with or without compensation), as we shall have to do in the case of the big landowners. Our task relative to the small peasant consists, in the first place, in effecting a transition of his private enterprise and private possession to co-operative ones, not forcibly but by dint of example and the proffer of social assistance for this purpose. And then of course we shall have ample means of showing to the small peasant prospective advantages that must be obvious to him even today." (Engels, *The Peasant Question in France and Germany*, p. 17, Alexeyeva ed.; there are mistakes in the Russian translation. Original in the *Neue Zeit*.)[35]

TACTICS
OF THE CLASS STRUGGLE
OF THE PROLETARIAT

Having as early as 1844-45 examined one of the chief defects of the earlier materialism, namely, its inability to understand the conditions or appreciate the importance of practical revolutionary activity, Marx, along with his theoretical work, all his life devoted unrelaxed attention to the tactical problems of the class struggle of the proletariat. An immense amount of material bearing on this is contained in *all* the works of Marx and particularly in the four volumes of his correspondence with Engels published in 1913. This material is still far from having been assembled, collected, studied and examined. We shall therefore have to confine ourselves here to the most general and briefest remarks, emphasizing that Marx justly considered that without *t h i s* side to it materialism was irresolute, one-sided, and lifeless. Marx defined the fundamental task of proletarian tactics in strict conformity with all the postulates of his materialist-dialectical conception. Only an objective consideration of the sum-total of reciprocal relations of all the classes of a given society without exception, and, consequently, a consideration of the objective stage of development of that society and of the reciprocal relations between it and other societies, can serve as a basis for correct tactics of the advanced class. At the same time, all classes and all countries are regarded not statically, but dynamically, i.e., not in a state of immobility, but in motion (the laws of which are determined by the economic conditions of existence of each class). Motion, in its turn, is regarded not only from the standpoint of the past, but also from the standpoint of the future, and, at the same time, not in accordance with the vulgar conception of the "evolutionists," who see only slow changes, but dialectically: "in developments of such magnitude twenty years are no more than a day," Marx wrote to Engels, "though later on days may come again in which twenty years are concentrated." (*Briefwechsel*, Vol. III, p. 127.)[36] At each stage of development, at each moment, proletarian tactics must take account of this objectively inevitable dialectics of human history, on the one hand utilizing the periods of political stagnation or of sluggish, so-called "peaceful" development in order to develop the class consciousness, strength and fighting capacity of the advanced class, and, on the other hand, conducting all this work of utilization towards the "final aim" of the movement of this class and towards the creation in it of the faculty for practically performing great tasks in the great days in which "twenty years are concentrated." Two of Marx's arguments are of special importance in this connexion: one of these is contained in *The Poverty of Philosophy* and concerns the economic struggle and economic organizations of the proletariat; the other is contained in the *Communist Manifesto* and concerns the political tasks of the proletariat. The first argument runs as follows: "Large-scale industry concentrates in one place a crowd of people unknown to one another. Competition divides their interests. But the maintenance of wages, this common interest which they have against their boss, unites them in a common thought of resistance—combination. . . . Combinations, at first isolated, constitute themselves into groups . . . and in face of always united capital, the maintenance of the association becomes more necessary to them [i.e., the workers] than that of wages. . . . In this struggle— a veritable civil war—all the elements necessary for a coming battle unite and develop. Once it has reached this point, association takes on a political character."[37] Here we have the programme and tactics of the economic struggle and of the trade-union movement for several decades to come, for all the long period in which the proletariat will muster its forces for the "coming battle." Side by side with this must be placed numerous references by Marx and Engels to the example of the British labour movement; how industrial "prosperity" leads to attempts "to buy the workers" (*Briefwechsel*, Vol. I, p. 136),[38] to divert them from the struggle; how this prosperity generally "demoralizes the workers" (Vol. II, p. 218); how the British proletariat becomes "bourgeoisified"—"this most bourgeois of all nations is apparently aiming ultimately at the possession of a bourgeois aristocracy and a bourgeois proletariat as well as a bourgeoisie" (Vol. II, p. 290);[39] how its "revolutionary energy" oozes away (Vol. III, p. 124); how it will be necessary to wait a more or less long time before "the English workers will free themselves from their apparent bourgeois infection" (Vol. III, p. 127); how the British labour movement "lacks the mettle of the Chartists" (1866, Vol. III, p. 305);[40] how the British workers' leaders are becoming a type midway between "a radical bourgeois and a worker" (in reference to Holyoak, Vol. IV, p. 209); how, owing to British monopoly, and as long as this monopoly lasts, "the British workingman will not budge" (Vol. IV, p. 433).[41] The tactics of the economic struggle, in connexion with the general course *(and outcome)* of the labour movement, are here considered from a remarkably broad, comprehensive, dialectical, and genuinely revolutionary standpoint.

The *Communist Manifesto* set forth the fundamental Marxian principle on the tactics of the political struggle: "The Communists fight for the attainment of the immediate aims, for the enforcement of the momentary interests of the working class; but in the movement of the present, they also represent and take care of the future of that movement." That was why in 1848 Marx supported the party of the "agrarian revolution" in Poland, "that party which fomented the insurrection of Cracow in 1846."[42] In Germany in 1848 and 1849 Marx supported the extreme revolutionary democracy, and subsequently never retracted what he had then said about tactics. He regarded the German bourgeoisie as an element which was "inclined from the very beginning to betray the people" (only an alliance with the peasantry could have brought the bourgeoisie the integral fulfilment of its tasks) "and compromise with the crowned representatives of the old society."[43] Here is Marx's summary of the analysis of the class position of the German bourgeoisie in the era of the bourgeois-democratic revolution—an analysis which, incidentally, is a sample of that materialism which examines society in motion, and, moreover, not only from the side of the motion which is directed *backwards*: "Without faith in itself, without faith in the people, grumbling at those above, trembling before those below ...

intimidated by the world storm ... no energy in any respect, plagiarism in every respect ... without initiative ... an execrable old man, who saw himself doomed to guide and deflect the first youthful impulses of a robust people in his own senile interests. ...." (*Neue Rheinische Zeitung*, 1848; see *Literarischer Nachlass*, Vol. III, p. 212.) About twenty years later, in a letter to Engels (*Briefwechsel*, Vol. III, p. 224), Marx declared that the cause of the failure of the Revolution of 1848 was that the bourgeoisie had preferred peace with slavery to the mere prospect of a fight for freedom. When the revolutionary era of 1848-49 ended, Marx opposed every attempt to play at revolution (the fight he put up against Schapper and Willich), and insisted on ability to work in the new phase which in a seemingly "peaceful" way was preparing for new revolutions. The spirit in which Marx wanted the work to be carried on is shown by his estimate of the situation in Germany in 1856, the blackest period of reaction: "The whole thing in Germany will depend on the possibility of backing the proletarian revolution by some second edition of the Peasant War." (*Briefwechsel*, Vol. II, p. 108.)[44] As long as the democratic (bourgeois) revolution in Germany was not finished, Marx wholly concentrated attention in the tactics of the socialist proletariat on developing the democratic energy of the peasantry. He held that Lassalle's attitude was "objectively ... a betrayal of the whole workers' movement to Prussia" (Vol. III, p. 210), incidentally because Lassalle connived at the actions of the Junkers and Prussian nationalism. "In a predominantly agricultural country," wrote Engels in 1865, exchanging ideas with Marx on the subject of an intended joint statement by them in the press, "... it is dastardly to make an exclusive attack on the bourgeoisie in the name of the industrial proletariat but never to devote

a word to the patriarchal exploitation of the rural proletariat under the lash of the great feudal aristocracy."
(Vol. III, p. 217.)[45] From 1864 to 1870, when the era of
the completion of the bourgeois-democratic revolution
in Germany, the era of the efforts of the exploiting
classes of Prussia and Austria to complete this revolution in one way or another *from above*, was coming to
an end, Marx not only condemned Lassalle, who was
coquetting with Bismarck, but also corrected Lieb-
knecht, who had inclined towards "Austrophilism" and
the defence of particularism; Marx demanded revolutionary tactics which would combat both Bismarck and
the Austrophiles with equal ruthlessness, tactics which
would not be adapted to the "victor," the Prussian Jun-
ker, but which would immediately renew the revolutionary struggle against him *also on the basis* created
by the Prussian military victories. (*Briefwechsel*, Vol.
III, pp. 134, 136, 147, 179, 204, 210, 215, 418, 437, 440-
41.)[46] In the famous Address of the International of
September 9, 1870, Marx warned the French proletariat
against an untimely uprising; but when the uprising
nevertheless took place (1871), Marx enthusiastically
hailed the revolutionary initiative of the masses, who
were "storming heaven" (letter of Marx to Kugel-
mann). The defeat of the revolutionary action in this
situation, as in many others, was, from the standpoint
of Marxian dialectical materialism, a lesser evil in the
general course *and outcome* of the proletarian struggle
than the abandonment of a position already occupied,
than a surrender without battle. Such a surrender
would have demoralized the proletariat and undermined its fighting capacity. Fully appreciating the use
of legal means of struggle during periods when political
stagnation prevails and bourgeois legality dominates,
Marx, in 1877 and 1878, after the passage of the Anti-
Socialist Law,[47] sharply condemned Most's "revolution-

ary phrases"; but he no less, if not more sharply, attacked the opportunism that had temporarily gained sway in the official Social-Democratic Party, which did not at once display resoluteness, firmness, revolutionary spirit and a readiness to resort to an illegal struggle in response to the Anti-Socialist Law. (*Briefwechsel*, Vol. IV, pp. 397, 404, 418, 422, 424,[48] cf. also letters to Sorge.)

July-November, 1914
First published in 1915 in the *Granat Encyclopedia*, 7th edition, Vol. 28
Signed: *V. Ilyin*

Translated from V. I. Lenin's *Works*, 4th Russ. ed., Vol. 21, pp. 30-62

FREDERICK ENGELS[49]

Oh, what a lamp of reason ceased to burn,
Oh, what a heart then ceased to throb![50]

On August 5, 1895, Frederick Engels died in London. After his friend Karl Marx (who died in 1883), Engels was the most noteworthy scholar and teacher of the modern proletariat in all the civilized world. From the time that fate brought Karl Marx and Frederick Engels together, the life work of each of the two friends became the common cause of both. And so, to understand what Frederick Engels has done for the proletariat, one must have a clear idea of the significance of Marx's work and teaching for the development of the contemporary labour movement. Marx and Engels were the first to show that the working class and the demands of the working class are a necessary outcome of the present economic system, which together with the bourgeoisie inevitably creates and organizes the proletariat. They showed that it is not the well-meaning efforts of noble-minded individuals, but the class struggle of the organized proletariat that will deliver humanity from the evils which now oppress it. In their scientific works, Marx and Engels were the first to explain that socialism is not the invention of dreamers, but the final aim and inevitable result of the development of the productive forces of modern society. All recorded history hitherto has been a history of class struggle, of the succession of the rule and victory of certain social classes over others. And this will continue until the foundations of class struggle and of class rule—private property and anarchic social production—disappear. The interests of the proletariat demand the destruction of these foundations, and therefore the conscious class struggle of the organized workers must be directed against them. And every class struggle is a political struggle.

These views of Marx and Engels have now been adopted by all proletarians who are fighting for their emancipation. But when in the forties the two friends took part in the socialist literature and social movements of their time, such opinions were absolutely novel. At that time there were many people, talented and untalented, honest and dishonest, who, while absorbed in the struggle for political freedom, in the struggle against the despotism of monarchs, police and priests, failed to observe the antagonism between the interests of the bourgeoisie and the interests of the proletariat. These people would not even admit the idea that the workers should act as an independent social force. On the other hand, there were many dreamers, some of them geniuses, who thought that it was only necessary to convince the rulers and the governing classes of the injustice of the contemporary social order, and it would then be easy to establish peace and general well-being on earth. They dreamt of socialism without a struggle. Lastly, nearly all the Socialists of that time and the friends of the working class generally regarded the proletariat only as an *ulcer*, and observed with horror how this ulcer grew with the growth of industry. They all, therefore, were intent on how to stop the development of industry and of the proletariat, how to stop the "wheel of history." Far from sharing the general fear of the development of the proletariat, Marx and Engels placed all their hopes on the continued growth of the proletariat. The greater the number of proletarians, the greater would be their power as a revolutionary class, and the nearer and more possible would socialism become. The services rendered by Marx and Engels to the working class may be expressed in a few words thus: they taught the working class to know itself and be conscious of itself, and they substituted science for dreams.

That is why the name and life of Engels should be known to every worker. That is why in this collection of articles,[51] the aim of which, as of all our publications, is to awaken class consciousness in the Russian workers, we must sketch the life and work of Frederick Engels, one of the two great teachers of the modern proletariat.

Engels was born in 1820 in Barmen, in the Rhine province of the kingdom of Prussia. His father was a manufacturer. In 1838, Engels, without having completed his studies at the gymnasium, was forced by family circumstances to enter one of the commercial houses of Bremen as a clerk. Commercial affairs did not prevent Engels from pursuing his scientific and political education. He came to hate autocracy and the tyranny of bureaucrats while still at the gymnasium. The study of philosophy led him further. At that time Hegel's teaching dominated German philosophy, and Engels became his follower. Although Hegel himself was an admirer of the autocratic Prussian state, in whose service he stood as a professor in the University of Berlin, Hegel's *teaching* was revolutionary. Hegel's faith in human reason and its rights, and the fundamental thesis of the Hegelian philosophy, namely, that the universe is subject to a constant process of change and development, was leading those of the disciples of the Berlin philosopher who refused to reconcile themselves to the existing state of affairs to the idea that the struggle against this state of affairs, the struggle against existing wrong and prevalent evil, is also rooted in the universal law of eternal development. If all things develop, if institutions keep giving place to other institutions, why should the autocracy of the Prussian king or of the Russian tsar, why should the enrichment of an insignificant minority at the expense of the vast majority, or the domination of the bourgeoisie over the people, continue forever? Hegel's philosophy spoke of the development of the mind and of ideas; it was *idealistic*. From the development of the mind it deduced the development of nature, of man, and of human, social relations. Retaining Hegel's idea of the eternal process of development,* Marx and Engels rejected the preconceived idealist view; turning to the facts of life, they saw that it was not the development of mind that explained the development of nature but that, on the contrary, the explanation of mind must be derived from nature, from matter.... Unlike Hegel and the other Hegelians, Marx and Engels were materialists. Regarding the world and humanity materialistically, they perceived that just as material causes lie at the basis of all the phenomena of nature, so the development of human society is conditioned by the development of material, productive forces. On the development of productive forces depend the relations which men enter into one with another in the production of the things required for the satisfaction of human needs. And in these relations lies the explanation of all the

---

* Marx and Engels frequently pointed out that in their intellectual development they were very much indebted to the great German philosophers, particularly to Hegel. "Without German philosophy," Engels says, "there would have been no scientific socialism."[52]

phenomena of social life, human aspirations, ideas and laws. The development of productive forces creates social relations based upon private property, but now we see that this same development of the productive forces deprives the majority of their property and concentrates it in the hands of an insignificant minority. It destroys property, the basis of the modern social order, it itself strives towards the very aim which the Socialists have set themselves. All the Socialists have to do is to realize which of the social forces, owing to its position in modern society, is interested in bringing about socialism, and to impart to this force the consciousness of its interests and of its historical mission. This force is the proletariat. Engels got to know it in England, in the centre of British industry, Manchester, where he settled in 1842, entering the service of a commercial house of which his father was a shareholder. Here Engels did not merely sit in the factory office but wandered about the slums in which the workers were cooped up. He saw their poverty and misery with his own eyes. But he did not confine himself to personal observations. He read all that had been revealed before him on the condition of the British working class and carefully studied all the official documents he could lay his hands on. The fruit of these studies and observations was the book which appeared in 1845: *The Condition of the Working Class in England.* We have already mentioned the chief service rendered by Engels as the author of *The Condition of the Working Class in England.* Many even before Engels had described the sufferings of the proletariat and had pointed to the necessity of helping it. Engels was the *first* to say that *not only* was the proletariat a suffering class, but that, in fact, the disgraceful economic condition of the proletariat was driving it irresistibly forward and compelling it to fight for its ultimate emancipation. And the fighting proletariat *would help itself.* The political movement of the working class would inevitably lead the workers to realize that their only salvation lay in socialism. On the other hand, socialism would become a force only when it became the aim of the *political struggle of the working class.* Such are the main ideas of Engels's book on the condition of the working class in England, ideas which have now been adopted by all thinking and fighting proletarians, but which at that time were entirely new. These ideas were enunciated in a book which is written in an absorbing style and which is filled with most authentic and shocking pictures of the misery of the English proletariat. This book was a terrible indictment of capitalism and the bourgeoisie. It created a very profound impression. Engels's book began to be quoted everywhere as presenting the best picture of the condition of the modern proletariat. And, in fact, neither before 1845 nor after has there appeared so striking and truthful a picture of the misery of the working class.

It was not until he came to England that Engels became a Socialist. In Manchester he formed contacts with people active in the British labour movement at the time and began to write for English socialist publications. In 1844, while on his way back to Germany, he became acquainted in Paris with Marx, with whom he had already started a correspondence. In Paris, under the influence of the French Socialists and French life, Marx had also become a Socialist. Here the friends jointly wrote a book entitled *The Holy Family, or Critique of Critical Critique.* This book, which appeared a year before *The Condition of the Working Class in England,* and the greater part of which was written by Marx, contains the foundations of revolutionary materialist socialism, the main ideas of which we have expounded above. *The Holy Family* is a facetious nickname for the Bauer brothers, philosophers, and their followers. These gentlemen preached a criticism which stood above all reality, which stood above parties and politics, which rejected all practical activity, and which only "critically" contemplated the surrounding world and the events going on within it. These gentlemen, the Bauers, superciliously regarded the proletariat as an uncritical mass. Marx and Engels vigorously opposed this absurd and harmful trend. On behalf of a real human personality—the worker, trampled down by the ruling classes and the state—they demanded, not contemplation, but a struggle for a better order of society. They, of course, regarded the proletariat as the power that was capable of waging this struggle and that was interested in it. Even before the appearance of *The Holy Family*, Engels had published in Marx's and Ruge's *Deutsch-Französische Jahrbücher*[53] the "Critical Essays on Political Economy," in which he examined the principal phenomena of the contemporary economic order from a socialist standpoint and concluded that they were necessary consequences of the rule of private property. Intercourse with Engels was undoubtedly a factor in Marx's decision to study political economy, a science in which his works have produced a veritable revolution.

From 1845 to 1847 Engels lived in Brussels and Paris, combining scientific pursuits with practical activities among the German workers in Brussels and Paris. Here Marx and Engels formed contact with the secret German Communist League, which commissioned them to expound the main principles of the socialism they had worked out. Thus arose the famous *Manifesto of the Communist Party* of Marx and Engels, published in 1848. This little booklet is worth whole volumes: to this day its spirit inspires and motivates the organized and fighting proletariat of the entire civilized world.

The revolution of 1848, which broke out first in France and then spread to other countries of Western Europe, brought Marx and Engels back to their native country. Here, in Rhenish Prussia, they took charge of the democratic *Neue Rheinische Zeitung* published in Cologne. The two friends were the heart and soul of all revolutionary-democratic aspirations in Rhenish Prussia. They defended the interests of the people and of freedom against the reactionary forces to the last ditch. The reactionary forces, as we know, gained the upper hand. The *Neue Rheinische Zeitung* was suppressed. Marx, who during his exile had lost his Prussian citizenship, was deported; Engels took part in the armed popular uprising, fought for liberty in three battles, and after the defeat of the rebels fled, via Switzerland, to London.

There Marx also settled. Engels soon became a clerk once more, and later a shareholder, in the Manchester commercial house in which he had worked in the forties. Until 1870 he lived in Manchester, while Marx lived in London, which, however, did not prevent them maintaining a most lively intellectual intercourse: they corresponded almost daily. In this correspondence the two friends exchanged views and knowledge and continued to collaborate in the working out of scientific socialism. In 1870 Engels moved to London, and their common intellectual life, full of strenuous labour, continued until 1883, when Marx died. Its fruit was, on Marx's side, *Capital*, the greatest work on political economy of our age, and on Engels's side—a number of works, large and small. Marx worked on the analysis of the complex phenomena of capitalist economy. Engels, in simply written and frequently polemical works, dealt with the more general scientific problems and with diverse phenomena of the past and present in the spirit of the materialist conception of history and Marx's economic theory. Of these works of Engels we shall mention: the polemical work against Dühring (in which are analyzed highly important problems in the domain of philosophy, natural science and the social sciences),* *The Origin of the Family, Private Property and the State* (translated into Russian, published in St. Petersburg, 3rd ed., 1895). *Ludwig Feuerbach* (Russian translation with notes by G. Plekhanov, Geneva, 1892), an article on the foreign policy of the Russian government (translated into Russian in the Geneva *Sotsial-Demokrat*, Nos. 1 and 2),[55] remarkable articles on the housing question,[56] and finally, two small but very valuable articles on the economic development of Russia (*Frederick Engels on Russia*, translated into Russian by Vera Zasulich, Geneva, 1894).[57] Marx died before he could complete his vast work on capital. In the rough, however, it was already finished, and after the death of his friend, Engels undertook the onerous labour of preparing and publishing the second and third volumes of *Capital.* He published Volume II in 1885 and Volume III in 1894 (his death prevented the prepartion of Volume IV).[58] These two volumes entailed a vast amount of labour. Adler, the Austrian Social-Democrat, has rightly remarked that by publishing Volumes II and III of *Capital* Engels erected a majestic monument to the genius who had been his friend, a monument on which, without intending it, he indelibly carved his own name. And, indeed, these two volumes of *Capital* are the work of two men: Marx and Engels. Ancient stories contain many moving instances of friendship. The European proletariat may say that its science

---

* This is a wonderfully rich and instructive book.[54] Unfortunately, only a small portion of it, containing a historical outline of the development of socialism, has been translated into Russian. (*The Development of Scientific Socialism*, 2nd ed., Geneva, 1892.)

was created by two scholars and fighters, whose relations to each other surpassed the most moving stories of human friendship among the ancients. Engels always— and, on the whole, justly—placed himself after Marx. "In Marx's lifetime," he wrote to an old friend, "I played second fiddle."[59] His love for the living Marx, and his reverence for the memory of the dead Marx were limitless. In this stern fighter and strict thinker beat a deeply loving heart.

After the movement of 1848-49, Marx and Engels in exile did not occupy themselves with science alone. In 1864 Marx founded the International Workingmen's Association, and led this society for a whole decade. Engels also took an active part in its affairs. The work of the International Association, which, in accordance with Marx's idea, united proletarians of all countries, was of tremendous significance in the development of the working-class movement. But even after the International Association came to an end in the seventies the unifying role of Marx and Engels did not cease. On the contrary, it may be said that their importance as spiritual leaders of the labour movement steadily grew, inasmuch as the movement itself grew uninterruptedly. After the death of Marx, Engels continued alone to be the counsellor and leader of the European Socialists. His advice and directions were sought for equally by the German Socialists, who, despite government persecution, grew rapidly and steadily in strength, and by representatives of backward countries, such as Spaniards, Rumanians and Russians, who were obliged to ponder over and weigh their first steps. They all drew on the rich store of knowledge and experience of old Engels.

Marx and Engels, who both knew Russian and read Russian books, took a lively interest in Russia, followed the Russian revolutionary movement with sympathy and maintained contact with Russian revolutionaries. They were both *democrats* before they became Socialists, and the democratic feeling of *hatred* for political despotism was exceedingly strong in them. This direct political feeling, combined with a profound theoretical understanding of the connexion between political despotism and economic oppression, as well as their rich experience of life, made Marx and Engels uncommonly responsive precisely from the *political* standpoint. That is why the heroic struggle of the handful of Russian revolutionaries against the mighty tsarist government evoked a most sympathetic echo in the hearts of these tried revolutionaries. On the other hand, the tendency to turn away from the most immediate and important task of the Russian Socialists, namely, the conquest of political freedom, for the sake of illusory economic advantages, naturally appeared suspicious in their eyes and was even regarded by them as a direct betrayal of the great cause of the social revolution. "The emancipation of the proletariat must be the work of the proletariat itself"—Marx and Engels constantly taught. But in order to fight for its economic emancipation, the proletariat must win for itself certain *political* rights. Moreover, Marx and Engels clearly saw that a political revolution in Russia would be of tremendous significance to the West-European labour movement as well. Autocratic Russia had always been a bulwark of European reaction in general. The extraordinarily favourable international position enjoyed by Russia as a result of the war of 1870, which for a long time sowed discord between Germany and France, of course only enhanced the importance of autocratic Russia as a reactionary force. Only a free Russia, a Russia that had no need either to oppress the Poles, Finns, Germans, Armenians or any other small nations, or constantly to incite France and Germany against each other, would enable modern Europe to free itself from the burden of war, would weaken all the reactionary elements in Europe and would increase the power of the European working class. Engels therefore ardently desired the establishment of political freedom in Russia for the sake of the progress of the labour movement in the West as well. In him the Russian revolutionaries have lost their best friend.

May the memory of Frederick Engels, the great champion and teacher of the proletariat, live for ever!

Autumn, 1895

First published in the symposium *Rabotnik*, Nos. 1-2, 1896

Translated from V. I. Lenin's **Works**, 4th Russ. ed., Vol. 2, pp. 1-13

NOTES

1—Lenin's *Three Sources and Three Component Parts of Marxism* were published in the journal *Prosveshcheniye*, No. 3, 1913, dedicated to the 30th anniversary of Marx's death.

Prosveshcheniye (Enlightenment)—a Bolshevik socio-political and literary monthly published legally in St. Petersburg from December 1911 to June 1914. It was put out on Lenin's instructions in place of *Mysl (Thought)*, a Bolshevik monthly published in Moscow, which was banned by the tsarist authorities. Lenin guided *Prosveshcheniye* from abroad, edited articles for it, and corresponded regularly with the members of its editorial board. The journal published the following works by Lenin: *Fundamental Issues of the Election Campaign, The Three Sources and Three Component Parts of Marxism, Critical Remarks on the National Question, The Right of Nations to Self-Determination*, and others.

The editorial board consisted of M. A. Savelyev, M. S. Olminsky, A. I. Yelizarova, and others. The circulation of the journal rose to 5,000 copies. On the eve of the First World War it was banned by the authorities. *Prosveshcheniye* was resumed in the autumn of 1917 but just one (double) issue of it appeared, containing Lenin's works, *Can the Bolsheviks Retain State Power?* and *About Revision of the Party Programme*. p. 7

2—V. I. Lenin set out to write *Karl Marx* for the encyclopedic dictionary of the Granat Brothers Society in spring 1914 in Poronino, Galicia, and completed in November 1914 in Berne, Switzerland. In a preface written by Lenin when the article was published as a separate pamphlet, he from memory cites the year of writing as 1913.

The article appeared in the dictionary in 1915, signed by V. Ilyin and supplemented with a *Bibliography of Marxism*. For censorship reasons the editors deleted two chapters—*Socialism* and *Tactics of the Class Struggle of the Proletariat*—and made a few changes in the text.

In 1918 the Priboi Publishers put the work out in pamphlet form with Lenin's preface, just as it appeared in the dictionary, but omitting the *Bibliography of Marxism*.

The full text in accordance with the manuscript was first published in 1925 in a collection titled *Marx-Engels-Marxism*, prepared by the Lenin Institute of the Central Committee of the Russian Communist Party of Bolsheviks.

The present edition is without the bibliography.   p. 14

3—The present article was followed by a review of Marxist literature and literature about Marxism omitted in this edition.   p. 16

4—Allusion is made to Marx's statement in *The Critique of the Hegelian Philosophy of Right*.   p. 17

5—*The Communist League*—the first international communist organization of the proletariat. Its establishment was preceded by considerable spadework by Marx and Engels in rallying Socialists and foremost workers of various countries ideologically and organizationally. With this aim in view they organized the Communist Correspondence Committee in Brussels early in 1846. Marx and Engels defended the ideas of scientific communism in bitter controversies with the vulgar equalitarian communism advocated by Wilhelm Weitling, "true socialism" and the petty-bourgeois utopias of Proudhon, which had an influence, among other bodies, on members of the League of the Just—a secret society of workers and artisans which had lodges in Germany, France, Switzerland and Britain. The London leadership of the League of the Just, convinced in the justice of Marx's and Engels's ideas, invited them to join their organization late in January 1847 and take part in re-organizing it, and also in drafting a programme of the League based on principles which they set forth. Marx and Engels accepted the invitation.

The congress of the League of the Just held in London early in June 1847 has gone down in history as the first congress of the Communist League. Engels and Wilhelm Wolff took part in the congress. At the congress the League of the Just was renamed the Communist League and the old obscure slogan, "All Men Are Brothers," was replaced with the militant internationalist slogan of the proletarian party—"Workingmen of All Countries, Unite!" The congress also examined the "Rules of the Communist League," which Engels actively helped to draw up. The

new rules clearly defined the final goals of the communist movement and omitted clauses which lent the organization the
features of a secret society. The structure of the League was
based on democratic principles. Final approval of the rules came
at the second congress of the Communist League. Both Marx
and Engels took part in the second congress in London, November
29-December 8, 1847. In prolonged debates they upheld the principles of scientific communism, which were finally adopted by
the congress unanimously. It was at the request of the congress
that Marx and Engels wrote the *Manifesto of the Communist
Party*—this programmatic document made public in February
1848.

When the revolution broke out in France the Central Committee of the League, with its seat in London, turned over the
leadership late in February 1848 to the Brussels District Committee headed by Marx. After the latter was deported from Brussels and moved to Paris, the seat of the new Central Committee
was removed to the French capital early in March. Engels was
also elected to the Central Committee. In late March and early
April 1848 the Central Committee arranged for the repatriation
of a few hundred German workers, mostly members of the Communist League, to take part in the German revolution, which had
then begun. The political platform of the Communist League in
this revolution was set forth in the *Demands of the Communist
Party in Germany*, formulated by Marx and Engels late in March.

On arriving in Germany early in April 1848 Marx, Engels and
their followers realized that in backward Germany, where the
workers were disunited and insufficiently conscious politically,
the two or three hundred members of the Communist League
scattered throughout the country were unable to influence the
broad masses to any appreciable extent. As a consequence, Marx
and Engels saw fit to join the extreme, in effect proletarian, left
wing of the democratic movement. They joined the Cologne Democratic Society and recommended their followers to join democratic groups in order to uphold in them the standpoint of the
revolutionary proletariat, to criticize the inconsistency and vacil-
lation of petty-bourgeois democrats, and spur them to resolute
action. At the same time, Marx and Engels urged them to organize workers' societies, to concentrate on the political education of the proletariat, and to lay the foundations for a mass
proletarian party. The *Neue Rheinische Zeitung* edited by Marx
was the guiding centre for members of the Communist League.
Late in 1848 the League Central Committee in London tried to
restore contacts and sent Joseph Moll to Germany as an emis-

sary with the purpose of re-organizing the League. The London body had amended the 1847 rules, reducing their political impact. It was no longer the overthrow of the bourgeoisie, the establishment of proletarian rule and the. building of a classless communist society that were defined in them as the chief aims of the Communist League. Instead, they spoke of a social republic. Moll's mission in Germany in the winter of 1848-49 fell through.

In April 1849 Marx, Engels and their followers quit the Democratic Society. Now that the working masses had gained political experience and were bitterly disappointed in the petty-bourgeois democrats it was time to think of establishing an independent proletarian party. But Marx and Engels failed to carry out their plan. An uprising broke out in South-Western Germany, and its defeat put an end to the German revolution.

The course of the revolution revealed that the views of the Communist League, as set forth in the *Manifesto of the Communist Party*, were perfectly correct, and that the League was an excellent school of revolutionary skill. Its members participated with vigour in the movement, defending the standpoint of the proletariat, that most revolutionary class, in the press, on the barricades and in the battle-fields.

The defeat of the revolution was a painful blow to the Communist League. Many of its members were imprisoned or had emigrated. Addresses and contacts were lost. Local branches had ceased to function. The League also suffered considerable losses outside Germany.

In autumn 1849 most of the leaders of the League assembled in London. Thanks to the efforts of the new, re-organized Central Committee headed by Marx and Engels the former organization was restored and the activities of the League revived in spring 1850. The *Address of the Central Committee to the Communist League*, written by Marx and Engels in March 1850, summed up the results of the 1848-49 revolution and set the task of forming a proletarian party independent of the petty bourgeoisie. The *Address* was the first to define the idea of permanent revolution. A new communist organ came off the press in March 1850. It was the *Neue Rheinische Zeitung. Politisch-ökonomische Revue.*

In the summer of 1850 a controversy arose in the Central Committee of the Communist League over the question of tactics. A majority headed by Marx and Engels firmly opposed the faction of August Willich and Karl Schapper, who proposed the sectarian and reckless tactics of starting a revolution without delay, in total disregard of objective developments and the realities of the political situation in Europe. In the meantime, Marx and Engels laid prime emphasis on the propagation of scientific communism and the training of proletarian revolutionaries for forthcoming revolutionary clashes. This, they said, was the principal task of the Communist League at a time when the reactionaries had assumed the offensive. In mid-September 1850, the schismatic activities of the Willich-Schapper faction brought about a rupture. At a sitting on September 15 the powers of the Central Committee were transferred at Marx's suggestion to the Cologne District Committee. The Communist League branches in Germany approved this decision of the London Central Committee. On instructions from Marx and Engels, the new Central Committee in Cologne drew up a new set of League rules in December 1850. In May 1851, police persecution and arrests brought the activities of the Communist League in Germany to a virtual standstill. Soon after the Cologne Communist trial, Marx urged the Communist League to announce its dissolution. It did so on November 17, 1852.

The Communist League has done its historical share as a school of proletarian revolutionaries, the nucleus of a proletarian party, and the predecessor of the International Workingmen's Association—the First International. p. 17

6—*Neue Rheinische Zeitung. Organ der Demokratie*—a Cologne daily edited by Karl Marx; published from June 1, 1848 to May 19, 1849.

On returning to Germany after emigrating, Marx and Engels set out at once to realize their plan for a revolutionary organ of the press, which they regarded as a powerful means of influencing the masses. In view of the conditions obtaining in Germany at the time, Marx, Engels and their followers assumed the political standpoint of the Left, in effect proletarian, wing of the democratic movement. This predetermined the tendency of the *Neue Rheinische Zeitung*, which appeared with *Organ der Democratie* written into its masthead.

A militant organ of the proletarian wing of the democratic movement, the *Neue Rheinische Zeitung* served to educate the masses and rallied them to fight the counter-revolution. In its effort to keep its readers informed of all the important events of the German and European revolution, the paper often put out second editions. Whenever its four pages could not hold all the news, it published supplements, and whenever new important despatches came to hand it put out extra supplements and extra editions, which were printed in leaflet form. Editorials stating the attitude of the newspaper to the major issues of the revolution were, as a rule, written by Marx or Engels. These editorials are marked *Köln and **Köln. Articles marked with a single asterisk sometimes appeared in other sections of the paper (among despatches from Italy, France, Britain, Hungary, and other countries). Aside from handling the correspondence and helping the editor-in-chief in technical matters, each of the editors dealt with a limited, specific round of questions. Engels wrote critical reviews of debates in the Berlin and Frankfort national assemblies and the second chamber of the Prussian Landtag, articles about the revolutionary war in Hungary, the national-liberation movement in Italy, the war in Schleswig-Holstein and, between November 1848 and January 1849, a series of articles on Switzerland. Wilhelm Wolff wrote about the agrarian issue in the German revolution, the situation of the peasantry and the peasant movement, particularly in Silesia, and ran the section of current news, "In the Country." Georg Weerth ran the section of humour in rhyme and prose. Ernest Dronke was at one time the paper's correspondent in Frankfort-on-Main, wrote some articles about Poland, and in March-May 1849 reviews of reports from Italy. Ferdinand Wolff was for a long time correspondent of the paper in Paris. Heinrich Bürger's association with the paper confined itself, according to Marx and Engels, to a single article, which was furthermore radically revised by Marx. Ferdinand Freiligrath, who joined the editorial board in October 1848, contributed revolutionary verses.

The paper's determined and irreconcilable stand, its militant internationalism and the appearance in it of political exposés of the Prussian government and the local Cologne authorities—all this from the first caused it to be baited by the feudal-monarchist and liberal-bourgeois press and persecuted by the government. The authorities refused Marx the right to Prussian citizenship to prejudice his stay in the Rhine Province, and initiated court proceedings against the paper's editors, principally Marx and Engels. After the September events in Cologne the military authorities proclaimed martial law there on September 26, 1848, and banned a number of democratic publications, the Neue Rheinische Zeitung among them. Engels, Dronke and Ferdinand Wolff were compelled to leave Cologne temporarily to avoid arrest and Wilhelm Wolff had to go to the Pfalz for a few months, and then to hide from the police in Cologne itself. Owing to Engels's forced departure from Germany the brunt of the editorial work, including the writing of editorials, fell to Marx's share until January 1849.

In the teeth of persecutions and political obstructions the *Neue Rheinische Zeitung* courageously defended the interests of the revolutionary democrats and the proletariat. In May 1849, the time of a general counter-revolutionary offensive, the Prussian government took advantage of the fact that Marx was not granted Prussian citizenship to order his deportation. Marx's departure and repressions against the other editors of the paper caused it to cease publication. The last, 301st, issue of the *Neue Rheinische Zeitung*, printed in red, appeared on May 19, 1849. In a parting statement to the Cologne workers the editors declared that "their last word always and everywhere will be: liberation of the working class!" p. 18

7—See K. Marx, *Capital*, Vol. I, Moscow 1958, p. 19. p. 21

8—See F. Engels, *Anti-Dühring*, Moscow 1954, pp. 65-66, 86, 55, 38-39. p. 22

9—F. Engels, *Ludwig Feuerbach and the End of Classical German Philosophy*. See K. Marx and F. Engels, *Selected Works*, Vol. II, Moscow 1958, pp. 369, 370, 371. p. 22

10—Letter from K. Marx to F. Engels, December 12, 1866. p. 23

11—See F. Engels, *Anti-Dühring*, Moscow 1954, p. 158. p. 23

12—K. Marx, *Theses on Feuerbach*. See K. Marx and F. Engels, *Selected Works*, Vol. II, Moscow 1958, pp. 403-05. p. 23

13—See F. Engels, *Anti-Dühring*, Moscow 1954, pp. 17, 36. p. 24

14—F. Engels, *Ludwig Feuerbach and the End of Classical German Philosophy*. See K. Marx and F. Engels, *Selected Works*, Vol. II, Moscow 1958, pp. 386-87, 363, 387. p. 25

15—See F. Engels, *Anti-Dühring*, Moscow 1954, p. 40. p. 25

16—F. Engels, *Ludwig Feuerbach and the End of Classical German Philosophy*. See K. Marx and F. Engels, *Selected Works*, Vol. II, Moscow 1958, p. 376. p. 26

17—See K. Marx, *Capital*, Vol. I, Moscow 1958, p. 372. p. 26

18—See K. Marx and F. Engels, *Selected Works*, Vol. I, Moscow 1958, p. 363. p. 27

19—See K. Marx and F. Engels, *Selected Correspondence*, Moscow, p. 218. p. 27

20—See K. Marx and F. Engels, *Manifesto of the Communist Party*, Moscow 1957, pp. 47-48, 66. p. 31

21—See K. Marx and F. Engels, *Manifesto of the Communist Party*, Moscow 1957, p. 64. p. 31

22—See K. Marx, *Capital*, Vol. I, Moscow 1958, p. 10. p. 31

23—See K. Marx, *Capital*, Vol. I, Moscow 1958, p. 74. p. 33

24—K. Marx, *A Contribution to the Critique of Political Economy*. p. 33

25—See K. Marx, *Capital*, Vol. I, Moscow 1958, p. 170. p. 34

26—See K. Marx, *Capital*, Vol. I, Moscow 1958, p. 167. p. 35

27—See K. Marx, *Capital*, Vol. I, Moscow 1958, pp. 762, 763. p. 39

28—See K. Marx and F. Engels, *Selected Correspondence*, Moscow, pp. 157-62, 164-65. p. 42

29—See K. Marx, *Das Kapital*, Bd. III, Berlin 1953, S. 850. p. 43

30—See K. Marx, *Capital*, Vol. I, Moscow 1958, pp. 747, 642. p. 44

31—See K. Marx, *Das Kapital*, Bd. III, Berlin 1953, SS. 858, 859. p. 45

32—See K. Marx, *Capital*, Vol. I, Moscow 1958, pp. 506-07. p. 46

33—See K. Marx, *Capital*, Vol. I, Moscow 1958, pp. 489-90, 484. p. 48

34—See F. Engels, *Anti-Dühring*, Moscow 1954, p. 389. p. 49

35—See K. Marx and F. Engels, *Selected Works*, Vol. II, Moscow 1958, p. 433. p. 50

36—See K. Marx and F. Engels, *Selected Correspondence*, Moscow, p. 172. p. 51

37—See K. Marx, *The Poverty of Philosophy*, Moscow, pp. 194-95.   p. 52

38—Letter from F. Engels to K. Marx, February 5, 1854.   p. 52

39—Letter from F. Engels to K. Marx, October 7, 1858.   p. 52

40—Letter from F. Engels to K. Marx, April 8, 1863.
Letters from K. Marx to F. Engels, April 9, 1863 and April 2, 1866.   p. 52

41—Letters from F. Engels to K. Marx, November 19, 1869 and August 11, 1881.   p. 53

42—See K. Marx and F. Engels, *Manifesto of the Communist Party*, Moscow 1957, pp. 109, 110.   p. 53

43—See K. Marx, *Bourgeoisie and Counter-revolution*.   p. 53

44—See K. Marx and F. Engels, *Selected Correspondence*, Moscow, p. 111.   p. 54

45—Letters from F. Engels to K. Marx, January 27, 1865 and February 5, 1865.   p. 55

46—Letters from F. Engels to K. Marx, June 11, 1863; November 24, 1863; September 4, 1864; January 27, 1865; October 22, 1867; December 6, 1867.
Letters from K. Marx to F. Engels, June 12, 1863; December 10, 1864; February 3, 1865; December 17, 1867.   p. 55

47—*The Anti-Socialist Law* was enacted in Germany on October 21, 1878. It banned all the organizations of the Social-Democratic Party, mass organizations of workers, and the workers' press, made socialist literature subject to confiscation and caused persecutions of Social-Democrats. Under pressure of the mass workers' movement it was repealed on October 1, 1880.   p. 55

48—Letters from K. Marx to F. Engels, July 23, 1877; August 1, 1877; September 10, 1879.
Letters from F. Engels to K. Marx, August 20, 1879 and September 9, 1879.   p. 56

49—V. I. Lenin wrote *Frederick Engels* in autumn 1895. It was first published in March 1896 in the symposium *Rabotnik*, No. 1.

77

Rabotnik (The Worker)—a non-periodical symposium published abroad through 1896-99 by the League of Russian Social-Democrats. The initiator of the publication was Lenin. On April 25 (May 7), 1895, Lenin went abroad to establish contacts with the Emancipation of Labour group and to study the West-European workers' movement. In Switzerland he reached an agreement with G. V. Plekhanov, P. B. Axelrod and other members of the group about the issue and editing of the symposium. On returning to Russia in September 1895 Lenin made every effort to provide the symposium with articles and correspondence from Russia and to organize financial support for it.

Aside from *Frederick Engels*, Lenin wrote several other items for the first issue of the symposium.

All in all, there appeared six issues of *Rabotnik* in three volumes, and ten issues of *Listok Rabotnika (The Workers' Newssheet).* p. 57

50—The words of the epigraph to *Frederick Engels* were taken by Lenin from a poem by N. A. Nekrasov, *In Memory of Dobrolyubov.* p. 57

51—See Note 49. p. 59

52—See K. Marx and F. Engels, *Selected Works*, Vol. I, Moscow 1958, p. 652. p. 60

53—Lenin refers to *Deutsch-Französische Jahrbücher*, a journal founded by Marx jointly with A. Ruge in Paris. Only one number (double) of it appeared in 1844. (See p. 17 of this booklet.) p. 63

54—Lenin refers to F. Engels's *Anti-Dühring. Herr Eugen Dühring's Revolution in Science.* p. 65

55—*Sotsial-Demokrat*—a literary and political review published abroad in 1890-92 by the Emancipation of Labour group; just four issues appeared. Lenin refers to Engels's article "Foreign Policy of Russian Tsarism."

56—K. Marx and F. Engels, *Selected Works*, Vol. I, Moscow 1958, pp. 546-635. p. 65

57—F. Engels, *On Social Relations in Russia.* See K. Marx and F. Engels, *Selected Works*, Vol. II, Moscow 1958, pp. 49-61. p. 65

58—Fourth volume of *Capital*—this, in accordance with Engels's own statement, is what Lenin calls Marx's *Theories of Surplus-Value*, written in 1862-63. In the preface to *Capital*, Vol. II, Engels wrote: "After eliminating the numerous passages covered by Books II and III, I intend to publish the critical part of this manuscript (*Theories of Surplus-Value.—Ed.*) as *Capital*, Book IV." But death prevented Engels from carrying out his plan. The *Theories of Surplus-Value* were published in German as prepared for print by K. Kautsky in 1905-10. This edition violated the basic requirements of a scientific publication and contained a number of distortions of Marxist principles.

The Institute of Marxism-Leninism of the Central Committee of the C.P.S.U. is putting out a new edition of *Theories of Surplus-Value* (*Capital*, Vol. IV) in three parts in accordance with the manuscript of 1862-63 (K. Marx, *Theories of Surplus-Value* [*Capital*, Vol. IV], Part I, 1955; Part II, 1957). p. 65

59—Letter from Engels to J. Ph. Becker, October 15, 1884. p. 66

TO THE READER

The Foreign Languages Publishing House would be glad to have your opinion of the translation and the design of this book.

Please send all suggestions to 21, Zubovsky Boulevard, Moscow, U.S.S.R.

Printed in the Union of Soviet Socialist Republics

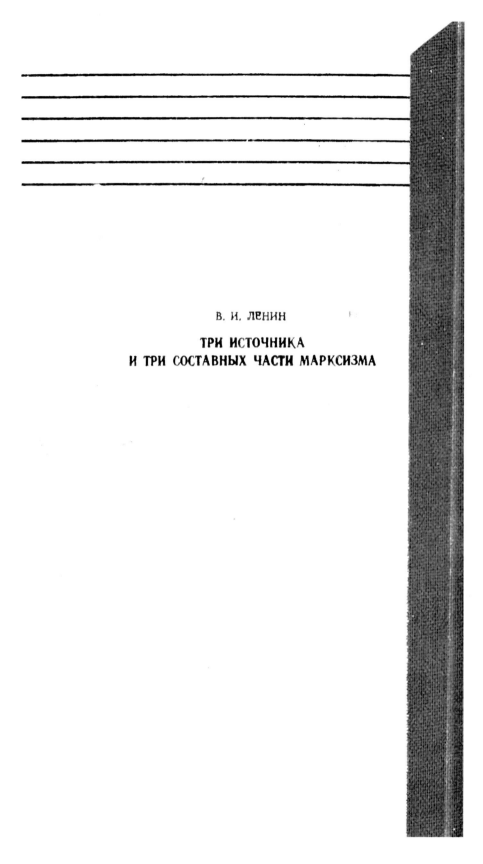

В. И. ЛЕНИН

**ТРИ ИСТОЧНИКА
И ТРИ СОСТАВНЫХ ЧАСТИ МАРКСИЗМА**

ImTheStory.com

Personalized Classic Books in many genre's

Unique gift for kids, partners, friends, colleagues

Customize:

- Character Names
- Upload your own front/back cover images (optional)
- Inscribe a personal message/dedication on the
  inside page (optional)

Customize many titles Including
- Alice in Wonderland
- Romeo and Juliet
- The Wizard of Oz
- A Christmas Carol
- Dracula
- Dr. Jekyll & Mr. Hyde
- And more...

CPSIA information can be obtained at www.ICGtesting.com
Printed in the USA
BVOW01s2254221113

337115BV00006B/29/P